DR. EUGENE UNDERWOOD

Attributes of Faith

First published by Life Publication: A Division of Spirit Life Ministries 2026

Formatting & Book Cover by Dr. M.L. Ellis

First edition

ISBN (print): 979-8-9868282-6-8
ISBN (digital): 979-8-9868282-7-5

This book was professionally typeset on Reedsy.
Find out more at reedsy.com

Contents

Foreword

Dr. Eugene Underwood is my best friend in Christ of many years and a prolific author of many books that are a blessing to the body of Christ. After reading this book, I am of the same impression that this book is also a blessing as well. This book covers the basics fundamentals of "Faith". He breaks down the different aspects of a walk of faith a believer needs to come into the full knowledge of the truth. Also, he gives you the real meat of "Faith" by establishing the depth that every believer needs especially for the ones who want to go beyond the veil. It is in this book, that he, Dr. Underwood, will give you the breath, the length, and depth concerning the type of "faith" that the Apostle Paul emphasized in Galatians 2:20 for those who want a "I'm crucified with Christ" understanding of "faith". So if you want to come to that hidden place of a revelation of faith, read this book, *Attributes of Faith,* and you will be blessed.

Pastor Leonard, H Barber,

His brother in Christ.

Preface

When I got born again at a young age, I walked away from God, but I came back to him right near the beginning of what we call the faith movement. I observed that many used faith as their personal rabbit's foot and named and claimed everything in sight. I saw so many abuses and shipwrecks of that which the bible calls our servant, which is faith. The bible says faith is a servant, but it is also a quality of our Father that he gives to his children to not only survive in this world but to walk in both kingdoms.

Our Father/Christ/Holy Spirit is a being who does not experience being alone. Though Our Father/Christ/Holy Spirit is one Being, He is also actually three Beings that fellowship with each other. For example, when Christ was on Planet Earth as Our Lord, He fellowshipped with Our Father in Heaven. (See John 17:20-23.) As Our Father and Christ are one, so Our Father and Holy Spirit are one. Since Our Father, Christ, and Holy Spirit are actually one, He does not experience being alone. The only time Our Father/Christ/Holy Spirit experienced being alone was when Christ cried out on the Cross, "My God, My God, why have you forsaken me?" The word forsaken means to leave alone. It was only in that one moment of time that Our Father/Christ/Holy Spirit experienced being alone. Since Our Father created us, humans in His image, it is His desire and plan that we not experience being alone. In the Garden of Eden, even though there were animals around Adam, he felt alone. So Our Father created Adam a helper companion,

Eve, so that Adam and all human beings following him would not have to be alone. (See Genesis 2:18.) One of the reasons Our Father created Adam as a man and Eve as a female was that the two would have needed to seek the companionship of each other and not be alone. One of the reasons that Our Father assigns Guardian or Ministering Angels to a born-again Christian is so that the person will not have to be alone. If you are a born-again Christian and living alone, you are not actually alone, as there are Guardian Angels with you, even though you cannot see them with your physical eyes. There is Biblical evidence that when Our Father assigns Guardian Angels, He assigns more than one. When the temptations by Satan of Our Lord were over, there were angels who ministered to Him. (See Matthew 4:11.) Psalm 91 is about one who is abiding in the secret place of the Most High as that one lives. In verse eleven, it is stated that Our Father gives charge or assigns angels to minister to that person. Angels are created beings, and as created beings, they are lower-rank beings than Our Father/Christ,/Holy Spirit. (See Psalm 148:2, 5 and Colossians 1:16.) We human beings are created lower rank beings than the angels. (See Psalm 8:3-8 and Hebrews 2:6-8.) Since the spirit light forms of angels and the spirit light forms of us humans living in our physical bodies come from Our Father, both the angels and we humans can have fellowship with Our Father/Christ,/Holy Spirit. There are two similar qualities in both the spirit being of Our Father/Christ/Holy Spirit and us Born Again Christians, so that we Born Again Christians can have fellowship with Our Father/Christ/Holy Spirit. These two elements are Love and Faith. We Born Again Christians know that Christians know that we will have fellowship with Our Father/Christ/Holy Spirit in Heaven, but we can have fellowship with Our Father/Christ/Holy Spirit as we live our lives on Planet Earth. This book begins with the Quality or Element of Faith. Apostle Paul says that our Father gives each one of us, born-again Christians, a Measure of Faith. One of the reasons for this Gift of Faith is to enable us to fellowship with Our Father/Christ,/Holy Spirit. The title of this book, "The Quality of Faith is also part of our beings and that of the lives of angels. I am aware of two verses of Scripture that support this statement. "Psalm 103:20 - 'Bless the Lord, you His angels, who excel in strength, who do His word, heeding the voice of His word'."Through the Quality of Faith in them, angels depend upon Our Father's Word. "Jude 9 – 'Yet Michael the archangel, in contending with the devil, when he disputed about the body of Moses, dared not bring against him a reviling accusation, but said, 'The Lord rebuke you!'- "When Archangel Michael argued with Satan, Archangel Michael only did what Our Father authorized him to do. It is the Quality of Faith that enables Archangel Michael, and the rest of the angels, the saints in Heaven, and born-again Christians on Planet Earth to respect the authority of Our Father.

I

I. The Quality of Faith

qual·i·ty
/ˈkwäləde̅/

the standard of something as measured against other things of a similar kind; the degree of excellence of something.

Chapter 1: The Quality of Faith

In our discussion of faith, we will cover the foundational fundamentals you are aware of, and much more. We will also build on the foundation you already have. When many hear the word "faith," they think of Christianity in general, as it relates to what they believe about the Bible or Christ. Some go a little further, not just what they believe, but how they can use it as a weapon in this fight against the enemy, and how to receive what they need in this world to survive. As we will see in our studies, faith is much more than that; its basics are how we relate to our Father, how he relates to us, and how he uses us in the battle against evil. From the quality of faith he gives us in our mother's womb, through our growing up in this world, to the age of accountability. From the measure of faith when we are born again to faith dunimas power that helps us overcome sin. Even to the gift of special faith that causes the believer to do exploits for our King, we will examine what many have ignored in this pursuit of our Father.

Consider this example: a child lives with its mother in her womb for nine months before it is born. During that time, the child gets to know the mother and develops trust in her care. The child also needs to develop the same trust in the father or others who care for them. Therefore, our Father gives a child procreated in a mother's womb a Quality of Faith. This faith enables the child to develop trust in their parents, allowing them to depend on their parents for survival. We call it intuition—the knowing that kids have at such a young age, like knowing how to suck a bottle and other things. Our Father calls it faith. Then a father comes alone after the baby is born and must earn the same trust and confidence the baby developed for the mother while living in the mother's womb.

A child learns to develop faith by trusting the parents who care for them every day, provided the child is not hurt or abused. In this way, when the child begins to grow up, praying to our Father with their parents, they learn to trust our Father at a very young age. This is the pattern our father chose.

Deuteronomy 7:9
(King James Version)
9 Know therefore that the Lord thy God, he is God, the faithful God, which keepeth covenant and mercy with them that love him and keep his commandments to a thousand generations;

1 Corinthians 1:9
(King James Version)
9 God is faithful, by whom ye were called unto the fellowship of his Son Jesus Christ our Lord.

2 Thessalonians 3:3

(King James Version)
3 But the Lord is faithful, who shall stablish you, and keep you from evil.

```
One way our Father will keep you from evil is to teach you
how to use your faith to develop trust in him and use faith
as a servant to fight the enemy.
```

1 John 1:9
(King James Version)
9 If we confess our sins, he is faithful and just to forgive us our sins, and to cleanse us from all unrighteousness.

This is one of the ways our Father teaches us to use our faith in the area of forgiveness. By using it, we keep ourselves free from the enemy's attacks, because sin removes us from under his protection, and repentance by faith covers us again. It also teaches us to forgive others by faith, regardless of how badly they hurt us. Therefore, faithfulness is one form of faith. This means that the Godhead has a quality of faith.

Genesis 1:26-27
(King James Version)
26 And God said, Let us make man in our image, after our likeness: and let them have dominion over the fish of the sea, and over the fowl of the air, and over the cattle, and over all the earth, and over every creeping thing that creepeth upon the earth.
27 So God created man in his own image, in the image of God created he him; male and female created he them.

Our Father created a human body for Adam that is similar to that of animals. But Our Father created a spirit being of Adam and placed the spirit being within the human body. The spirit being part was made in the likeness of Our Father. The spirit, being part of Adam, was a lesser light being form than that of Our Father but had the same qualities as that of Our Father. All procreated human beings since Adam are made like Adam. This means that every human being procreated in a mother's womb has a Quality of Faith like that of Our Father. This is why it is proper to say that every human being who is born already has a Quality of Faith within him or her."

Angels do not have a sin quality about them like humans or even like Born Again Christians. Evil did not start until those whom you know as Satan and fallen angels were cast out of Heaven. The sin factor did not become part of the lives of angels that did not fall, but it did in your lives. The sin factor did not enter human existence until Adam sinned in the Garden of Eden. Since that time, each human being has been born with a quality of sin in one's spiritual being, living in one's physical body. Therefore, humans have a sin factor that hinders the faith factor within them, but angels do not. Keep in mind, as we move further in our discussion, that Christ taught that the faith of all born-again Christians should function as a child's faith. Though a child has the factor of sin in his or her spirit being, that child is innocent of that sin. The spirit of a child is as though it is as white as snow, so the sin factor does not hinder the functioning of the quality of faith in a child.

THE SIN FACTOR

Isaiah 1:18
(King James Version)
18 Come now, and let us reason together, saith the Lord: though your sins be as scarlet, they shall be as white as snow; though they be red like crimson, they shall be as wool.

Mark 10:15
(King James Version)
15 Verily I say unto you, Whosoever shall not receive the kingdom of God as a little child, he shall not enter therein.

The word for child that Holy Spirit had the Apostle Mark use in his writing means an infant only a few days old. Actually, the word refers to a boy child who is nursed by his mother and is not yet at the age of circumcision. Since such a baby is born with an element of faith in his spirit being, his faith would function at that time. There are two qualities of faith of such a child that adult Born Again Christians should have. First of all, the child is so Young that all he is concerned about is depending on his mother to provide for his needs. Our Father desires that even you, adults, have this simple, childlike trust in Your Heavenly Father.

Secondly, though the child of this age also had a sin factor in his spirit, Our Father considered him innocent of that sin, and that sin did not hinder his simple faith in his mother. (So, the secret is to come to the father in childlikeness, and the sin factor in you will not affect your faith.)

Matthew 14:31
(King James Version)
31 And immediately Jesus stretched forth his hand, and caught him, and said unto him, O thou of little faith, wherefore didst thou doubt?

After Apostle Peter took a few steps on the water toward Jesus, he noticed the wind and the waves, became afraid, and sank into the water. When Jesus saved him, He told Apostle Peter he had little faith or doubt. Holy Spirit had Apostle Matthew use a word in his writing that means to waiver or temporarily not use the Quality of Faith within one. The real reason this happened to Apostle Peter was that he still had some influence from the quality of sin in his life. This was evident when Apostle Peter three times denied that he was a disciple of Your Lord on the night of the betrayal.

John 3:3
(King James Version)
3 Jesus answered and said unto him, Verily, verily, I say unto thee, Except a man be born again, he cannot see the kingdom of God.

The verb form that Holy Spirit had Apostle John use in this verse is a word that does not include the time factor. This means that being born anew from above, that is, becoming a Born-Again Christian, begins when a person decides to recognize Christ as Savior and confess and repent of sin. Though the action is complete, it is also one that a person must continue to perform. This means that Born-Again Christians will be overcoming the sin factor in their lives until they go to Heaven. Using the topic of persecution, Your Lord taught us about this when He was on planet Earth. (See Matthew 10:22.) Your Lord taught that because Born Again, Christians will have to face persecution, one's salvation would not be totally completed until the end of his or her life on Planet Earth. As long as a Born-Again Christian is living on Planet Earth, that one will need to be disciplining the sin factor within him or her so that the faith factor can function.

THE QUALITY OF FAITH AT WORK

Let me give you another example you may not have considered when it comes to the quality of faith we are speaking of. When children start walking and their parents instruct them on how to take steps, the child's initiative is a quality of faith at work. What am I saying? Many Born Again Christians feel that the quality of faith within you is for the purpose of the spirit being living within your human bodies. Our Father wants you to know that the faith within you should also be used in the development of your physical bodies. Faith can be a part of being a born-again Christian and keeping your body healthy. Faith can be a part of Born-Again Christians developing the talents and abilities Our Father has placed in their human bodies. I used my faith to learn my trade as a plumber, pipefitter, and welder before my father called me to preach, and I learned it extremely well and fast because of my faith, just as the three Hebrew boys did with their faith in captivity.

There is a caution to note. There are some people, including some Born Again Christians, who are putting more emphasis upon the care of their physical bodies than they are on caring for the spirit being living in their physical bodies. This is not a proper use of the Quality of Faith."

Mark 6:3
(King James Version)

3 Is not this the carpenter, the son of Mary, the brother of James, and Joses, and of Juda, and Simon? and are not his sisters here with us? And they were offended at him.

Luke 2:52

(King James Version)

52 And Jesus increased in wisdom and stature, and in favour with God and man.

In the verse in Apostle Mark's writing, Holy Spirit recorded that Your Lord was a carpenter. The writings of the four Gospels clearly show how he used the Quality of Faith within Him to develop the spirit living in His physical body. This verse also shows that your Lord used His faith to develop his physical body, including learning a trade. After his father died, He was the town carpenter before He became a preacher. The twelve disciples that Your Lord called had trained in trades or occupations. Apostle Paul trained himself to be a tentmaker. Your physical body, of course, is not more important than you as a spirit being living in your physical body.

But the Quality of Faith within you is for providing life both for you as a spirit being and for the physical body in which you are living. This is one thing that many do not discern as young believers, because they are only thinking of faith in retrospect, as getting something from God, rather than training themselves up in the ways of God, both naturally and spiritually.

CHAPTER 1: THE QUALITY OF FAITH

* * *

Chapter 2: The Quality of Faith (Part 2)

Our Father placed you as a spirit-being with a Quality of Faith into the human body conceived in your mother's womb. As you know, the purpose of this Quality of Faith is to let you, as a human being, have a relationship with the Godhead. This was your Miracle Day, your first experience of being born on Planet Earth. Nine months later, you moved outside of your mother's womb, and from the time that your parents realized that you had been conceived in your mother's womb, those who were born again and knew you were a gift from God. They began to take on the responsibility for the quality of faith in your spirit. Their goal was to lead you in such a way that someday you would make the decision to accept Christ as your Personal Savior and personally become responsible for the quality of faith in your spirit when you accepted Christ and accepted the Quality of Faith within you as your responsibility. This was the second time that you were born on Planet Earth. The first time you were born was both a physical and a spiritual birth in your mother's womb. The second time you were born was a totally spiritual experience. Our Father in

Heaven directed the experience, and it was new because you were now personally beginning to overcome the sin in your life. (This is why it is called the life of the overcomer.)

Of course, this is not the plan most families on Planet Earth follow, but those who do have more meaningful lives. For example, Our Father is better able to use your life because there has not been any time in your life when the faith quality within you has not been directed to Our Father, first by your parents and then by you. (I'm talking about those who taught their children and led them to Christ before the age of accountability). Now, let us consider another example. Suppose the parents of a child do not develop the faith quality in a child towards Our Father, and that person is well into his or her adult years of life before he or she begins to direct their faith towards Our Father. Such a person has many more memories and effects of sin in his or her life that must be taken care of before Our Father can use that person." (This is why I say, as a parent, you can make the father's job easier or harder.)

Matthew 1:21
(King James Version)
21 And she shall bring forth a son, and thou shalt call his name Jesus: for he shall save his people from their sins.

```
The word "bring forth" is a translation of one of the words
(HS) used in the New Testament, meaning "being born." This
word refers to the act of a mother giving birth to a son or
daughter.
```

John 3:7

(King James Version)
7 Marvel not that I said unto thee, Ye must be born again.

These are words that your Lord used in teaching a grown man by the name of Nicodemus. The word born means to be born as a son or daughter of Our Father and as a son or daughter of a man. Nicodemus understood that he had been born once as a son of Our Father and as a son of a man. Nicodemus had taken on the responsibility of the faith quality within him to do the commands of Our Father, so that he could worship Our Father. At first, Nicodemus was puzzled, as he knew that he could not again enter into his mother's womb. Then the Lord explained that He was referring to the spirit part of the first time he was born. His spirit being had a need to be born a second time as he accepted Your Lord as His Personal Savior and began to overcome the sin factor in his life as he continued to obey the commands of Our Father.

Our Father's Chosen People realize that there needs to be a time in each child's life when the child accepts responsibility for his or her spiritual life. They have the Bar Mitzvah ceremony in which the child is considered an adult and responsible for his or her spiritual life. They do this at the age of 13 for a boy and at the age of 12 for a girl. "For anyone who wants to get to Heaven, there needs to be an experience where that person realizes that he or she personally is responsible for the faith quality in their spirit being."

THE FAITH OF A CHILD

The reason your Lord taught about having faith like a child is that there are times when a child depends entirely on his or her parents. There are actions that occur before the Quality of Faith in a spirit living in a physical body functions, and actions that occur after the Quality of Faith functions. But when the Quality of Faith is functioning, there is always a time when the person is totally depending upon Our Father.

Deuteronomy 6:4-9
(King James Version)
4 Hear, O Israel: The Lord our God is one Lord:
5 And thou shalt love the Lord thy God with all thine heart, and with all thy soul, and with all thy might.
6 And these words, which I command thee this day, shall be in thine heart:
7 And thou shalt teach them diligently unto thy children, and shalt talk of them when thou sittest in thine house, and when thou walkest by the way, and when thou liest down, and when thou risest up.
8 And thou shalt bind them for a sign upon thine hand, and they shall be as frontlets between thine eyes.
9 And thou shalt write them upon the posts of thy house, and on thy gates.

Romans 10:14
(King James Version)
14 How then shall they call on him in whom they have not believed? and how shall they believe in him of whom they have not heard? and how shall they hear without a preacher?

I IN THEM AND THEY IN ME

Our Father has a plan that is often not followed. Our Father's plan is for parents to use the Quality of Faith within them to teach their children the commands and promises of Our Father. The parents are to keep doing this until their children mature to the point where they begin to realize that they are responsible for their own Christian life. Then the parents are to see that Holy Spirit has the opportunity to lead the child to use the Quality Faith to decide to repent, confess sin, and accept Jesus as one's Personal Savior. Our father's plan is that this decision be made when one is still a child and totally dependent on one's parents. Such a child can more easily begin to understand what it means to depend upon Our Father. There is something else Our Father wants you to be aware of. When you express your faith in depending upon Our Father, and this results in the faith quality of Our Father coming together with your faith, there is a sense in which Our Father is in You through the presence of Your Lord in You, but there is also a sense in which you are also in Him.

Revelation 3:20
(King James Version)
20 Behold, I stand at the door, and knock: if any man hear my voice, and open the door, I will come in to him, and will sup with him, and he with me.

Galatians 3:27
(King James Version)
27 For as many of you as have been baptized into Christ have put on Christ.

The Greek word for baptize that Holy Spirit had used in this verse is

baptidzo. The other word for baptism in the New Testament, used by Holy Spirit, is ***bapto***. (The word dipped in Revelation 19:13.) I am going to explain something very important by using the example of the pickle-making process. Of course, the first thing you would do would be to wash the pickled vegetables. Then you would prepare two pans of hot water on the stove. One pan is a pan of boiling water, and the other pan has boiling water with vinegar and other spices. Then dip (bapto) the pickle vegetables into the boiling water to kill all the germs or sterilize the pickle vegetables. Finally, you would put the pickled vegetables (baptidzo) into the pan of boiling water, vinegar, and other spices. Then you let the pickle vegetables simmer in the mixture for so many minutes that they turn into pickles.

HOW FAITH GROWS OR BECOMES ONE

This is a parable of what Our Lord intends to happen when the Quality of Faith in the spirit being of a person reaches out and begins to depend upon the Quality of Faith in Our Father. (Your faith and the father's faith come together) Not only does the person's outward life change, but one also begins to look like Christ in the way he or she lives. There is also an inward change that takes place, and one becomes like Our Father within one's ~ inner spirit. The best time for this to take place in the life of a person is that time in life when he or she realizes that he or she is responsible for the destiny of his or her soul." (What has mostly been left out in the teaching of faith is the quality of faith our father puts in every human to believe in him when taught, and then you extend your faith toward our father, then his faith takes over as it mixes with yours and gets the job done. Whether that faith was used to get you born again or healed or get your needs met, this is the pattern and this is how it works and grows.)

Remember, we told you that when Jesus taught, it meant you, Born Again Christians, should have faith like a very young child, a baby. The example that Holy Spirit used was a baby nursing in the arms of his mother before he was circumcised. This is important to understand as we begin to teach about some things that can be added to a child's life after that young infant age, which will hinder the proper functioning of the faith factor in the spirit being of the child or person. Because we live in a world that makes such a big deal of color, we lose what our father intended for us to be. We equate color to everything but what it was intended to be; it separates us, entitles us, and impoverishes us. If it were not for greed, there would not be any poverty in the land today. Then that impoverishment is based upon color. Even though we humans may have different skin colors, the spirit living in each of us is a light form being. We are all the same in this manner.

This is an important truth to keep in mind to understand what it means to have faith like a child. When a baby is still nursing in his or her mother's arms, the baby does not have any understanding of the different colors of human skin. What happens is that when the parents, Churches, and society begin to teach children about the different colors of skin, many times, there are prejudices that are taught along with the education. Not only are the children sometimes taught these prejudices, but they are also permitted to experience these prejudices. These prejudices always hinder the proper function of the Quality of Faith that is within each human being." "Prejudices will continue to increase, that is, worsen, until the time of Antichrist, and then increase or worsen even more during the time of Antichrist. This is to be expected in the world, but in some situations, it is also happening in some of Your Lord's Churches. This will continue until Your Lord Raptures (snatches away) His Church.

IN CHRIST THERE IS NO COLOR

Acts 10:34-35
(King James Version)
34 Then Peter opened his mouth, and said, Of a truth I perceive that God is no respecter of persons:
35 But in every nation he that feareth him, and worketh righteousness, is accepted with him.

In the time period of the Book of Acts, Holy Spirit arranged a meeting between Apostle Peter and a man named Cornelius, who was not of Apostle Peter's nation or race. While Apostle Peter was talking to this man, Holy Spirit impressed Apostle Peter that Our Father was sharing the same Favor of His Grace with Cornelius that He was sharing with Apostle Peter. "There is no partiality in the being of Our Father. He shares the total Favor of His Grace with anyone who fears Him. Since there is no partiality in Our Father, there is something that needs to be understood about His Chosen People. What happened is that Our Father extended a calling to those of the Old Testament who are referred to as Our Father's Chosen People. Our Father's plan was that His Chosen people receive the Favor of Our Father's Grace and then share the Favor of Our Father's Grace with all people of the world. Therefore, the source of prejudice is not Our Father. Let's continue to look at the faith of a child.

Even though the main interest of a baby nursing in his or her mother's arms is survival, that child actually learns deceitfulness and dishonesty from one's parents or peers. The faith quality with which a child is born can be trained to be either truthful and honest or deceitful and dishonest. Even though there is a sin quality in the spirit being of a child, Our Father will so take care of that child so that he or she will learn to be either honest or dishonest as taught by his or her parents or peers. Here is a verse of Scripture that contains a list of things that are not a part of a child's faith when a child is born and birthed, but are qualities that can be learned from a child's parents and peers.

FAITH THAT IS VOID

Revelation 22:15
(King James Version)
15 For without are dogs, and sorcerers, and whoremongers, and murderers, and idolaters, and whosoever loveth and maketh a lie.

People who accept Christ as Savior and do the commandments will be in Heaven. Those who do the things listed in this verse when they experience physical death will not go to Heaven. The other thing to note is that the things on this list are not part of the quality or makeup of Our Father, so these are not qualities in the Quality of Faith that Our Father places in the spirit being of each human being. "In the Bible, Holy Spirit used the term dog differently. One meaning of the word is a person who is greedy and grasping for money. Sometimes the person will do violence to obtain money. Such violence will make the receiver of the violence afraid of the one who does the violence. A child learns to be afraid of other human beings; it is not part of the Quality of Faith Our Father places in the child. The fear of a mother who has been raped can be transferred to her child. When a father abuses his son, that child can be as afraid of Our Father as he is of his earthly father. A child learns this type of fear, which hinders the proper function of the Quality of Faith within a child. "Sorcerers are people who use magical remedies. Occult practices always hinder the proper use of the Quality of Faith Our Father places in a person.

The Greek word used for sexually immoral is the word from which pornography comes. Pornography, female and male prostitution, adultery, and homosexuality are things that are learned and hinder the proper use of the Quality of Faith placed in a person by Our Father. Murder also hinders the proper use of the Quality of Faith. This includes killing with a weapon, killing with words, and abortion. "The term idolatry is also about something that hinders the proper use of the faith quality. This is about worshipping other gods, including the god of mammon. "The final thing on the list is to lie. Again, a child learns this from his or her parents or peers. The Quality of Faith cannot function properly if a person tells lies and is deceitful."

Our Father created humans with a quality that is to function as your imagination when you are a child. There are two parts to this quality of imagination that is part of you when you are created as a child. (As you well know, this is a big part of a child's life and serves as a form of communication.) However, because we don't understand it completely, we abandon it when we grow up because the enemy captures it because of our lack of understanding, and we squash it.) First, after you become a born-again Christian, the purpose is no longer imagination. The Holy Spirit uses this quality to give you dreams and visions. (See Acts 2:17.) Secondly, this part of the Quality of Faith I am referring to as imagination was designed by Our Father so that a child can learn how Our Father speaks to humans through it. Did you notice anything about this part of the Quality of Faith after you became a Born-Again Christian?" Psychologists refer to this quality as fantasy. Holy Spirit has not actually given this part of your Quality of Faith a name. Still, it is part of the Quality of Faith in human beings that enables you to have conversations with Our Father/Christ/Holy Spirit when you become a Born-Again Christian." In a nutshell, it is used one way as a child and another way as an adult.

THE IMAGINATION OF FAITH

Matthew 11:17
(King James Version)
17 And saying, We have piped unto you, and ye have not danced; we have mourned unto you, and ye have not lamented.

This verse includes a parable about children in the time of the Lord on Planet Earth, playing a funeral procession and a wedding celebration. In this, your Lord recognized the pretending or imagination part of a child's faith quality or attribute. This should begin to function in a child's life when he or she is born and birthed." In the new birth, it takes on a different quality that our father does not name. This is why it is hard for Christians to discern when our father is speaking to them because it has not been properly trained, that part of you or your imagination that functioned when you were a child, but changed when you became a born-again child.

1 Samuel 3:9-10
(King James Version)
9 Therefore Eli said unto Samuel, Go, lie down: and it shall be, if he call thee, that thou shalt say, Speak, Lord; for thy servant heareth. So Samuel went and lay down in his place.
10 And the Lord came, and stood, and called as at other times, Samuel, Samuel. Then Samuel answered, Speak; for thy servant heareth.

Notice that our father did not force himself into the child's life. He waited until he opened the door. When he ran and told Eli, he could have simply said, "You're imagining it. Since he was a child, this was a part of his faith our father was accessing. "This is an example of the Element of Faith Our Father put within you when you were born in your mother's womb to function after you become a Born-Again Christian. Not only did that quality of faith give you the courage or faith to believe the Word to accept your Lord as your Savior, but it also gave you the courage to seek new truths in the Bible. Each Born Again Christian needs to continue to realize that as long as you are living in your physical bodies, there will always be more Bible truths for you to understand."

Romans 12:2

(King James Version)

2 And be not conformed to this world: but be ye transformed by the renewing of your mind, that ye may prove what is that good, and acceptable, and perfect, will of God.

In this verse, the only thing to consider is what Holy Spirit means by renewing the mind. By mind, he means the Quality of Faith ability that Our Father placed in you when you were born in your mother's womb, that gives you the ability to receive and record ideas in your mind and live your life based on the ideas. (By the word renewing, he means you should constantly change your mind to something better. This idea of renewal involves renovating a building to make it better.

Acts 17:10-11

(King James Version)

10 And the brethren immediately sent away Paul and Silas by night unto Berea: who coming thither went into the synagogue of the Jews.

11 These were more noble than those in Thessalonica, in that they received the word with all readiness of mind, and searched the scriptures daily, whether those things were so.

This Bible example is the proper way to renew your mind as a born-again Christian. The brethren at Berea listened intently, eager to learn new truth, and remembered what Paul and Silas said to them. Then they went to the Scriptures and searched them to see whether what Paul and Silas said was Scriptural truth. This is a good example to follow. If one says that he or she is called of Our Father to share Our Father's Word, listen intently to what the person says. It is even good to take notes so you will not forget what was said. Then, search the Bible and let Holy Spirit tell you whether or not what you heard is Bible truth."

Romans 1:28

(King James Version)

28 And even as they did not like to retain God in their knowledge, God gave them over to a reprobate mind, to do those things which are not convenient;

One meaning of the word reprobate is that a reprobate idea occurs when a Born-Again Christian accepts an idea without testing it on the Scriptures.

* * *

II

II. The Age of Decision Making

de·ci·sion

/dəˈsiZH(ə)n/

a conclusion or resolution reached after consideration.

Chapter 3: The Age of Decision Making

If you remember, I mentioned that at the age of twelve or thirteen, I discovered that my faith quality included the ability to decide, such as surrendering my life to the Lord. When I was born in my mother's womb, a part of the faith quality Our Father placed in my spirit being was the ability to make decisions concerning the spirit being living in my physical body. The first time I made a decision was when I realized I had the ability and responsibility to decide to become a born-again Christian. Of course, I did not know about the age of accountability until many years later.

The faith quality that Our Father places in the spirit beings of humans when you are born in your mother's womb matures after you are born. This maturing takes place under the direction of one's parents, or someone doing the role of one's parents, teachers, and peers. Our Father plans that, at the average age of twelve for girls and thirteen for boys, they will already be taught that they have a spirit living in their physical bodies. Also, at this age, they are to realize that up to this point in their lives, their parents have been responsible for their spirit beings, but now each one is responsible for his or her spirit being.

Our Father's plan is that while the spirit being in a child is under the responsibility of that one's parents, Our Father communicates to the child that He is the creator. (See Romans 1:19-20.) According to Our Father's plan, when the child is old enough to understand that Our Father is the creator, he or she will want to worship Our Father. Our Father's plan is that at the Age of Decision Making, each child chooses _to worship Our Father. Again, those in the role of parents, teachers, and peers are complicating Our Father's plan as many are teaching about other religions, idols, self-worship, and Satan worship. When a child comes to the Age of Decision Making, each child will decide based on what he or she has been taught. The Age of Decision Making begins in each child, and he or she will choose to begin to worship the Godhead or some other god, an idol, self, or Satan. This is because of the Quality of Faith Our Father placed or places in each one born in his or her mother's womb." Now you understand why humans seek something to worship.

Joshua 24:15-17
(King James Version)
15 And if it seem evil unto you to serve the Lord, choose you this day whom ye will serve; whether the gods which your fathers served that were on the other side of the flood, or the gods of the Amorites, in whose land ye dwell: but as for me and my house, we will serve the Lord.
16 And the people answered and said, God forbid that we should forsake the Lord, to serve other gods;
17 For the Lord our God, he it is that brought us up and our

fathers out of the land of Egypt, from the house of bondage, and which did those great signs in our sight, and preserved us in all the way wherein we went, and among all the people through whom we passed:

```
The Age of Decision Making began for Joshua and our Father's
Chosen People when they were twelve and thirteen years of
age. In this event, they are adults and making decisions
about whether to serve and worship Our Father or other gods
and idols."
```

1 John 1:8-10
(King James Version)
8 If we say that we have no sin, we deceive ourselves, and the truth is not in us.
9 If we confess our sins, he is faithful and just to forgive us our sins, and to cleanse us from all unrighteousness.
10 If we say that we have not sinned, we make him a liar, and his word is not in us.

THE CHOICE IS YOURS

Born Again Christians in this Church Age of Our Lord should still be using the decision-making ability in the faith quality placed in them when they were born into their mother's womb. For example, the same attitudes and spirits that will make Antichrist what he will be when he becomes ruler of Planet Earth are already present on Planet Earth. You have the ability of faith to choose to follow Our Father rather than the Spirit of Antichrist. Using this decision-making ability should be an important part of the faith experience of each of you, Born Again Christians." Our Father created you with the ability to know the difference between good and evil and make decisions to do good rather than evil. This ability is part of the faith quality that Our Father placed within your spirit being when you were born in your mother's womb. I have a question. How do you define good and evil?" "Good is Our Father and His actions. When I am part of Our Father's actions, I am doing good things. Evil is Satan and his actions. If I were to do Satan's things, I would be doing evil things.

Matthew 4:1-11
(King James Version)

4 Then was Jesus led up of the Spirit into the wilderness to be tempted of the devil.
2 And when he had fasted forty days and forty nights, he was afterward an hungred.
3 And when the tempter came to him, he said, If thou be the Son of God, command that these stones be made bread.
4 But he answered and said, It is written, Man shall not live by bread alone, but by every word that proceedeth out of the mouth of God.
5 Then the devil taketh him up into the holy city, and setteth him on a pinnacle of the temple,
6 And saith unto him, If thou be the Son of God, cast thyself down: for it is written, He shall give his angels charge concerning thee: and in their hands they shall bear thee up, lest at any time thou dash thy foot against a stone.
7 Jesus said unto him, It is written again, Thou shalt not tempt the Lord thy God.
8 Again, the devil taketh him up into an exceeding high mountain, and sheweth him all the kingdoms of the world, and the glory of them;

9 And saith unto him, All these things will I give thee, if thou wilt fall down and worship me.
10 Then saith Jesus unto him, Get thee hence, Satan: for it is written, Thou shalt worship the Lord thy God, and him only shalt thou serve.
11 Then the devil leaveth him, and, behold, angels came and ministered unto him.

Matthew 6:13

(King James Version)

13 And lead us not into temptation, but deliver us from evil: For thine is the kingdom, and the power, and the glory, for ever. Amen.

When our Lord was on Planet Earth living in a human body, he recognized that there was an Evil One, Satan, who did evil things. This is true even though some teachers and professors tried to convince me otherwise.

Genesis 2:17

(King James Version)

17 But of the tree of the knowledge of good and evil, thou shalt not eat of it: for in the day that thou eatest thereof thou shalt surely die.

Genesis 3:22

(King James Version)

22 And the Lord God said, Behold, the man is become as one of us, to know good and evil: and now, lest he put forth his hand, and take also of the tree of life, and eat, and live for ever.

THE SEPARATION OF GOOD AND EVIL

At the end of the Great Millennium, Our Father will make a final separation between the good people and the evil people, as well as between the good angels and the evil angels. The good ones will live in Heaven and the evil ones in Hell. This means that part of Our Father's makeup is the ability to decide what is good and what is evil. This means that as Adam was created in the likeness of Our Father, in the faith quality placed in Adam, there was the ability for Adam to make decisions about what was good and what was evil. When Adam first lived in the Garden of Eden, he lived in a place where there was no evil. After Adam disobeyed Our Father and sinned, he was placed outside the Garden of Eden. He then had to live in places where evil existed. Adam became like Our Father/Christ/Holy Spirit in that he had to decide what was good and what was evil, and a fallen person can decide it to be whatever they want, but you must have Our Father inside you and his word to know which is which.

Numbers 13:32-33
(King James Version)

32 And they brought up an evil report of the land which they had searched unto the children of Israel, saying, The land, through which we have gone to search it, is a land that eateth up the inhabitants thereof; and all the people that we saw in it are men of a great stature.
33 And there we saw the giants, the sons of Anak, which come of the giants: and we were in our own sight as grasshoppers, and so we were in their sight.

Of the twelve spies sent into the Promised Land to evaluate it, they gave reports upon their return that were considered evil. What they gave were reports of exaggeration. Even though some of the people in the Promised Land were giants about nine or ten feet tall, the ten spies certainly gave an exaggerated report when they stated that Our Father's Chosen People were like grasshoppers compared to those living in the Promised Land. These ten spies could decide between the truth and a lie, but they chose to exaggerate the report into a lie. These ten spies did not properly use the faith quality Our Father had placed in them when they were born in their mothers' wombs."

Sometimes, when humans discuss the topic of good and evil, they use the terms light or white to refer to good and darkness or black to refer to evil. Some infer that much of what goes on in our society is a mixture of good and evil, or what people call a gray area. From this area of gray, the term "white lie" was born. As you well know, any form of a lie breaks the eighth commandment.

* * *

Chapter 4: The Age of Decision Making (Part 2)

Deuteronomy 5:20
(King James Version)
20 Neither shalt thou bear false witness against thy neighbour.

The Quality of Faith that Our Father placed in you when you were born in your mother's womb is not equipped to function based upon what some refer to as a gray area. You need to continue to define the events and issues of life in accordance with the laws of Our Father regarding how you act toward them. Your conscience is made to alert you to good, light, evil, or darkness. Your conscience will not help you very much if you decide that an issue or event is a gray area. Though one goal of Satan is to mix good and evil, our Father will always separate good and evil. "It is very true that many events you go into or places you go will have a combination of both good and evil. For example, there are times when, in living your ordinary life, you will find yourself in a place or places of evil or darkness. But note this, you can be the good or light in a dark place. Light always replaces darkness. Darkness happens only when light is removed. Your conscience is equipped to help you be light in dark places.

There is another aspect about how the Quality of Faith Our Father placed in your spirit being when you were born in your mother's womb, concerning the age of decision making as it relates to the matter of authority. As angels are also created beings, they respect authority. One example is recorded in Jude 9, when the Archangel Michael had a dispute with Satan: he did only what he had authority to do. "There is something else to note. As you know, Our Father is a spirit light form being. He used some of the energy in His being and engraved the Ten Commandments on two stone tablets with His finger.

Deuteronomy 9:9-10
(King James Version)
9 When I was gone up into the mount to receive the tables of stone, even the tables of the covenant which the Lord made with you, then I abode in the mount forty days and forty nights, I neither did eat bread nor drink water:
10 And the Lord delivered unto me two tables of stone written with the finger of God; and on them was written according to all the words, which the Lord spake with you in the mount out of the midst of the fire in the day of the assembly.

Exodus 24:4
(King James Version)
4 And Moses wrote all the words of the Lord, and rose up early in the morning, and builded an altar under the hill, and twelve pillars, according to the twelve tribes of Israel.

RECOGNIZING OUR FATHER'S AUTHORITY

As you know, before Our Father created the element of time, the only life quality or thing in existence was Our Father/Christ/Holy Spirit. Then, out of the life energy in Him, He began to create. He created the angels. Later, He created the universe in which Planet Earth exists, all the things on Planet Earth, and all the life forms on Planet Earth. (See Genesis 1:1-2:25.) I have a question for you. When an individual invents something, who has the best understanding or authority to write the rules or guidelines for its use? The person who made the invention has the best understanding of how to make the rules and regulations for using his or her invention." "Since Our Father is the one who created Planet Earth, all life forms, and all things on Planet Earth, He is the one who has the best understanding or authority to write the rules or regulations for His creation. For example. When you were born in your mother's womb, Our Father placed a Quality of Faith within your spirit being that has the capability of recognizing and accepting the authority of Our Father. If the Quality of Faith within you is to function properly, you must accept the truth that Our Father is your Creator.

Our Father began to give the rules and regulations for His creation when He wrote the Ten Commandments on two stone tablets. Then, he gave Patriarch Moses many other commandments and rules that Patriarch Moses had written down. These are the guidelines for a meaningful life. Our Father also has a plan for how these rules are to be shared with the people of His creation. There is a line of authority that Our Father follows. All this authority means is that Our Father has given some people the responsibility of sharing the rules. There are three areas of authority in the plan of Our Father to share His rules for His creation.

HOW THIS AUTHORITY IS MADE KNOWN

Of course, Holy Spirit is involved in one of the ways. Then, the father and/or husband of a family is to see that his family has the opportunity to learn the rules of Our Father. According to Deuteronomy 11:18-21 and Ephesians 5:23, Holy Spirit guides fathers in doing this, and Holy Spirit also gives some understanding of Our Father's rules to anyone who studies them in the Bible. Secondly, Your Lord gives apostles, prophets, evangelists, pastors, and teachers in His Body, His Church, the responsibility of sharing the rules of Our Father with Our Lord's Church. The third line of authority Our Father uses is that of the governments of the world. (See Romans 13:1-3.) The only time a Born-Again Christian does not have to obey a law of his or her government is when keeping the law would require the Born-Again Christian to violate one of Our Father's laws or rules. It should be noted that many people on Planet Earth suffer persecution for following this guideline. This is one of the reasons that Your Lord taught when living on Planet Earth, 'Blessed are those who are persecuted for righteousness' sake, for theirs is the kingdom of Heaven.' (See Matthew 5:10.)"

As I have stated, Our Father has placed within each human a Quality of Faith so that you can follow and depend upon his authority plan of Our Father. Another term to note is 'rebellion'. Rebellion is when one chooses not to follow the rules of Our Father. Sometimes a person decides to follow rules that he or she thinks come from a false god. Sometimes a person decides to make up their own rules for life. This is what Satan did while he was in Heaven, known as Lucifer or Day Star. When he did this, he had to be cast out of Heaven (See Isaiah 14:12-15.) When a person decides to make up his or her own rules for life, that person usually ends up letting Satan be the authority in his or her life. (See 1 Samuel 15:23.)"

It is the Quality of Faith that Our Father places in each human when you are born in your mother's womb that enables you to choose to follow these natural laws of Our Father or to disobey them. There are also some spiritual laws that Our Father has made, and each human has the choice of whether they will obey or disobey these spiritual laws. "There is one very important spiritual law Our Father gave before the Ten Commandments: the law of family. Our Father knew that Adam could not find the companionship he needed from the other life forms Our Father had created on Planet Earth, so He created Adam a helper companion. (See Genesis 2:18, 20-24.) With Adam and Eve being the first husband and wife, Our Father created His law of family. One man is to leave his parents, and one woman is to leave her parents. This one man and one woman are to become helper mates in a marriage relationship. There are two points to note. First of all, in Our Father's law for family, the priority is not having children; the priority is for the husband and wife to be helper mates to each other. *Secondly, Our Father's law does not include the idea of two men becoming helper mates or two women becoming helper mates. Again, with the Quality of Faith placed by Our Father in humans when you are born in your mother's womb, you choose whether or not you are going to obey or disobey his spiritual laws.

THE BASICS OF OUR FATHER'S LAWS

The Ten Commandments are the basis for all of Our Father's spiritual laws, so the Ten Commandments are very important. There is another point to note about Our Father's spiritual laws in the Ten Commandments. We looked at how Our Father, using the Spirit Light Energy in His being, used one of His fingers and engraved the Ten Commandments in two tablets of stone. (See again Deuteronomy 9:9-

10.) The other spiritual laws Our Father gave to Patriarch Moses, he wrote down. The reason Our Father wrote the Ten Commandments in stone by Himself is to show that the Ten Commandments are spiritual laws that humans are not to change, and they will be commandments in effect until the end of the Great Millennium. Therefore, we should only be trying to understand and make decisions to obey the spiritual laws."

Matthew 26:36-44
(King James Version)

36 Then cometh Jesus with them unto a place called Gethsemane, and saith unto the disciples, Sit ye here, while I go and pray yonder.
37 And he took with him Peter and the two sons of Zebedee, and began to be sorrowful and very heavy.
38 Then saith he unto them, My soul is exceeding sorrowful, even unto death: tarry ye here, and watch with me.
39 And he went a little farther, and fell on his face, and prayed, saying, O my Father, if it be possible, let this cup pass from me: nevertheless not as I will, but as thou wilt.
40 And he cometh unto the disciples, and findeth them asleep, and saith unto Peter, What, could ye not watch with me one hour?
41 Watch and pray, that ye enter not into temptation: the spirit indeed is willing, but the flesh is weak.
42 He went away again the second time, and prayed, saying, O my Father, if this cup may not pass away from me, except I drink it, thy will be done.
43 And he came and found them asleep again: for their eyes were heavy.
44 And he left them, and went away again, and prayed the third time, saying the same words.

Matthew 26:51-56

(King James Version)

51 And, behold, one of them which were with Jesus stretched out his hand, and drew his sword, and struck a servant of the high priest's, and smote off his ear.

52 Then said Jesus unto him, Put up again thy sword into his place: for all they that take the sword shall perish with the sword.

53 Thinkest thou that I cannot now pray to my Father, and he shall presently give me more than twelve legions of angels?

54 But how then shall the scriptures be fulfilled, that thus it must be?

55 In that same hour said Jesus to the multitudes, Are ye come out as against a thief with swords and staves for to take me? I sat daily with you teaching in the temple, and ye laid no hold on me.

56 But all this was done, that the scriptures of the prophets might be fulfilled. Then all the disciples forsook him, and fled.

While Your Lord was living in His human body on Planet Earth, He obeyed His Father by submitting His will to the will of His Father. You can also use your Quality of Faith to submit your will to Our Father in such a way that His will becomes the priority will factor in your life.

Hebrews 5:7-10

(King James Version)

7 Who in the days of his flesh, when he had offered up prayers and supplications with strong crying and tears unto him that was able to save him from death, and was heard in that he feared;

8 Though he were a Son, yet learned he obedience by the things which he suffered;

9 And being made perfect, he became the author of eternal salvation unto all them that obey him;

10 Called of God an high priest after the order of Melchisedec.

I know we cannot fully understand why or how it happened to the Lord, but He learned the deeper meaning of obedience when He endured the sufferings of the Cross. So, it is with you as a human being who is a Born-Again Christian, there are many things you can learn about being obedient to Our Father in your times of suffering.

Philippians 2:5-11
(King James Version)
5 Let this mind be in you, which was also in Christ Jesus:
6 Who, being in the form of God, thought it not robbery to be equal with God:
7 But made himself of no reputation, and took upon him the form of a servant, and was made in the likeness of men:
8 And being found in fashion as a man, he humbled himself, and became obedient unto death, even the death of the cross.
9 Wherefore God also hath highly exalted him, and given him a name which is above every name:
10 That at the name of Jesus every knee should bow, of things in heaven, and things in earth, and things under the earth;
11 And that every tongue should confess that Jesus Christ is Lord, to the glory of God the Father.

Your Lord was obedient to His Father when He came down from Heaven to earth and began to live in a physical body; He continued being obedient to His Father throughout His earthly life and His physical death experience on the Cross. The faith quality Our Father placed in you when you were born in your mother's womb is of such a nature that you can continue to choose to be obedient to Our Father to either your time of physical death or the Rapture of Your Lord's Church takes place.

FAITH AND CONSCIENCE

When you were born in your mother's womb, the quality of faith that our Father placed in your spirit includes a conscience. Before you matured to the Age of Decision Making, one of the reasons your parents taught you the Word of Our Father was to train your conscience. After you matured to the Age of Decision Making, you have been training your conscience with the Word of Our Father. As you learned the laws of Our Father, you were also training your conscience. Now your conscience functions as an alarm within you. Your conscience does two things for you. Your conscience lets you know when you are doing something good according to the laws of Our Father, and also when you are doing something bad according to the laws of Our Father.

John 8:9
(King James Version)
9 And they which heard it, being convicted by their own conscience, went out one by one, beginning at the eldest, even unto the last: and Jesus was left alone, and the woman standing in the midst.

The faith quality Our Father placed within you when you were born in your mother's womb enables you to know the difference between good and evil. Your conscience, part of that faith quality placed in you, enables you not only to distinguish between good and evil but also to make self-judgments of whether you are doing good or evil. You make these self-judgments based on your values and the laws of Our Father you have learned. In this verse of Scripture, these men who brought a woman to your Lord and accused the woman of adultery, made self-judgments of themselves that they were also sinners who were doing evil. When you do something good that is based upon your values from knowing the laws of Our Father, you will feel pleasure. When you do something that does not match these values, you will feel guilty. This is one of the most valuable tools our father has given you; don't sin it away or destroy your conscience's sensitivity.

1 Timothy 1:5
(King James Version)
5 Now the end of the commandment is charity out of a pure heart, and of a good conscience, and of faith unfeigned:

All who have been forgiven of the guilt of their sins and are training themselves to live according to the laws of our Father have what Timothy calls a good conscience.

Hebrews 10:22
(King James Version)
22 Let us draw near with a true heart in full assurance of faith, having our hearts sprinkled from an evil conscience, and our bodies washed with pure water.

A person has an evil conscience when the person has not yet been forgiven of sin, has not been taught the laws of Our

Father, and has made the decision not to give Our Father's laws priority in his or her life.

1 Corinthians 8:7
(King James Version)
7 Howbeit there is not in every man that knowledge: for some with conscience of the idol unto this hour eat it as a thing offered unto an idol; and their conscience being weak is defiled.

Titus 1:15
(King James Version)
15 Unto the pure all things are pure: but unto them that are defiled and unbelieving is nothing pure; but even their mind and conscience is defiled.

Idol worship or trying to worship Our Father and idols at the same time results in one having a weak and defiled conscience. One example is a Born-Again Christian who is doing the laws of Our Father but also finding pleasure in doing the things of the world. Moral impurity, including the physical union of a man and woman other than that of this union taking place between a man and woman in a marriage relationship, results in a weak and defiled conscience. This includes pornography."

1 Timothy 4:1-2
(King James Version)
4 Now the Spirit speaketh expressly, that in the latter times some shall depart from the faith, giving heed to seducing spirits, and doctrines of devils;

2 Speaking lies in hypocrisy; having their conscience seared with a hot iron;

2 Timothy 2:26
(King James Version)
26 And that they may recover themselves out of the snare of the devil, who are taken captive by him at his will.

```
Doing the things of Satan, such as magic, occult practices,
and horoscopes, results in a seared conscience. A seared
conscience is when a person knows the laws of Our Father,
but their conscience is not able to sound the alarm.
```

As Born-Again Christians who are living in human bodies in a natural world, there are times when you become so busy with your physical bodies and natural world that you forget about spiritual matters. The conscience that Our Father placed in each of you at your birth in your mother's womb can serve as an attention-getter in this matter. If your consciences are trained with the Word of Our Father, in the times when you are so busy that you tend to forget about spiritual matters, your conscience will alert you if you are at the point of beginning to do something bad or evil. It is important for you to study Scripture, but it is also important for you to study other things for survival in your physical bodies and the natural world. If the Word of Our Father trains your consciences, and if a born-again Christian begins to consider accepting a bad or evil idea, their conscience will alert them. This differs from (HS) Gift of Discerning of Spirits, which is discerning the spirits of Our Father, Satan, and self."

James 1:25

(King James Version)
25 But whoso looketh into the perfect law of liberty, and continueth therein, he being not a forgetful hearer, but a doer of the work, this man shall be blessed in his deed.

Hebrews 13:16
(King James Version)
16 But to do good and to communicate forget not: for with such sacrifices God is well pleased.

Even though you are a born-again Christian, there are times when you are so busy or tired that your recall from your memory is not as good or fast as it should be. This is referred to as forgetfulness. Since your conscience is trained with the Word of Our Father, you should be able to decide whether an idea coming to your mind is good or evil. But sometimes your recall of Scripture is a little slow, and your decision is hindered. In times like this, your conscience will alert you to any evil ideas coming to your mind until your recall can function and you remember what the Scripture says about the idea." This is why it is important to keep sin out of your life and practice waiting on God.

Matthew 5:27-30
(King James Version)
27 Ye have heard that it was said by them of old time, Thou shalt not commit adultery:
28 But I say unto you, That whosoever looketh on a woman to lust after her hath committed adultery with her already in his heart.
29 And if thy right eye offend thee, pluck it out, and cast it from thee: for it is profitable for thee that one of thy members should perish, and not that thy whole body should

be cast into hell.
30 And if thy right hand offend thee, cut it off, and cast it from thee: for it is profitable for thee that one of thy members should perish, and not that thy whole body should be cast into hell.

Demons like to hide in the light images of the pictures of violence, greed, and sex that you take into your being through your eyes. Even though you may carefully screen your television viewing, other than religious telecasts, almost every program you view has some elements of violence, greed, and sex. This is true even in most commercials. You find that since you have trained your conscience with the Word of Our Father, it immediately alerts you when you begin to view such pictures on television. This gives you the opportunity not to receive the light images coming from your television that could have some demons hiding in the light images of violence, greed, and sex.

Born Again Christians must know that guilt should only continue until one asks for forgiveness for a sin. You have heard some of the expressions of some Born Again Christians that are a sign that there may be some ongoing guilt in the person. For example, 1) I feel inferior as a person when I am in the presence of some people.' 2) 'There are many Christians who are much better Christians than I am.' 3) 'I am not good enough and I do not have the ability to do the ministry Our Father wants me to do.

All of you born-again Christians should realize that if Our Father is as great as you say He is, none of your shortcomings or mistakes will ever hinder Our Father from doing His will and purpose. There is a daily renewal of faith that Holy Spirit suggests take place for each one of you, Born Again Christians. First of all, begin each day with the understanding that Our Father is so great that He can have each of you be the person He wants you to be. Secondly, ask Holy Spirit to reveal any changes in your lives that Our Father wants you to make, and he will reveal these changes when they should take place. Thirdly, each day, ask Our Father if there are any changes to be made today so that I can be the person You want me to be tomorrow. If you do this, Satan will not be able to keep an ongoing guilt in your life that will depress you, make you feel inferior, or pull you down in life."

In John nine, this is an example of when the leaders of a man's religion did some things that gave Satan the opportunity to put some of this long-term guilt in the inner being of the man. All you need to know about the age of the man is that he was old enough to be a beggar at the entrance of the Temple. Based upon the question that the disciples asked Your Lord, it is evident that this man had been taught that he was born as a blind man because either he had sinned after he was born in his mother's womb, or his parents had committed some sin. This was a basis for long-term guilt. After the man received his miracle, the religious leaders tried to make him feel guilty for being healed on the Sabbath Day, but this man was not going to be part of any long-term guilt anymore. All guilt was gone because a few hours earlier he was blind, but now he could see, and he knew that Our Father had brought about his healing."

John 8:1-12
(King James Version)
8 Jesus went unto the mount of Olives.
2 And early in the morning he came again into the temple, and all the people came unto him; and he sat down, and taught them.
3 And the scribes and Pharisees brought unto him a woman

***taken in adultery; and when they had set her in the midst,
4 They say unto him, Master, this woman was taken in
adultery, in the very act.
5 Now Moses in the law commanded us, that such should be
stoned: but what sayest thou?
6 This they said, tempting him, that they might have to
accuse him. But Jesus stooped down, and with his finger
wrote on the ground, as though he heard them not.
7 So when they continued asking him, he lifted up himself,
and said unto them, He that is without sin among you, let
him first cast a stone at her.
8 And again he stooped down, and wrote on the ground.
9 And they which heard it, being convicted by their own
conscience, went out one by one, beginning at the eldest,
even unto the last: and Jesus was left alone, and the woman
standing in the midst.
10 When Jesus had lifted up himself, and saw none but the
woman, he said unto her, Woman, where are those thine
accusers? hath no man condemned thee?
11 She said, No man, Lord. And Jesus said unto her, Neither
do I condemn thee: go, and sin no more.
12 Then spake Jesus again unto them, saying, I am the light
of the world: he that followeth me shall not walk in
darkness, but shall have the light of life.***

A group of men brought a lady to your Lord, whom some of them had caught in an act of adultery. In the process of your Lord ministering to the lady, each one of these men began to feel guilty because of their own sins. But they did not come to your Lord to receive forgiveness of sin and freedom from guilt. One by one, they left with their guilt.

* * *

III

III. The Measure of Faith

meas·ure
/ˈmeZHər/

ascertain the size, amount, or degree of (something) by using an instrument or device marked in standard units or by comparing it with an object of known size.

Chapter 5: The Measure of Faith

When translators translate the word pistos as a noun, it refers to what a person knows about Our Father and the laws of Our Father. When the word pistos is translated as a verb, it means to believe or live one's life based upon what one knows about Our Father and the laws of Our Father.

Romans 12:1-3
(King James Version)
12 I beseech you therefore, brethren, by the mercies of God,
that ye present your bodies a living sacrifice, holy,
acceptable unto God, which is your reasonable service.
2 And be not conformed to this world: but be ye transformed
by the renewing of your mind, that ye may prove what is
that good, and acceptable, and perfect, will of God.
3 For I say, through the grace given unto me, to every man
that is among you, not to think of himself more highly than
he ought to think; but to think soberly, according as God

hath dealt to every man the measure of faith.

The foundation of faith is knowing that Our Father is a being or person of faith or faithfulness. (See again Deuteronomy 7:9, 1 Corinthians 1:9, 2 Thessalonians 3:3, 1 John 1:9.)

Deuteronomy 7:9
(King James Version)
9 Know therefore that the Lord thy God, he is God, the faithful God, which keepeth covenant and mercy with them that love him and keep his commandments to a thousand generations;

1 Corinthians 1:9
(King James Version)
9 God is faithful, by whom ye were called unto the fellowship of his Son Jesus Christ our Lord.

2 Thessalonians 3:3
(King James Version)
3 But the Lord is faithful, who shall stablish you, and keep you from evil.

1 John 1:9
(King James Version)
9 If we confess our sins, he is faithful and just to forgive us our sins, and to cleanse us from all unrighteousness.

Faith begins by knowing that Our Father is the Creator of Planet Earth, the universe of Planet Earth, and all the living beings and things on Earth. Faith is knowing that when you were born in your mother's womb that Our Father placed a Quality of Faith made in His image or likeness within your spirit being in Your physical body "Faith is knowing that just like an inventor is the one who knows how his or her invention can be operated, so Our Father is the one who knows how His creation can function for the purpose He intends. Our Father has natural laws for the universe and Planet Earth, physical laws for human bodies, and spiritual laws for the spirit being living in your physical body. You can learn the natural laws from the Bible and other sources; you can learn the physical laws from the Bible and other sources, but you can learn the spiritual laws only from the Bible. Faith is knowing that the laws of Our Father, written in the Bible, are called the Word of Our Father. Faith is knowing that when you were born from your mother's womb, your parents started to teach you the natural, physical, and spiritual laws of Our Father. Faith is also knowing that your parents taught you how to believe, that is, to live your life based on the natural, physical, and spiritual laws of Our Father.

Faith is knowing that because you were hearing the Word of Our Father in preaching and teaching, when you became the Age of Choosing, Holy Spirit was able to lead you to ask for forgiveness of your sin and become a Born-Again Christian. According to Romans 12:3, when you became a born-again Christian, our Father gave you the free Gift of His Grace. Faith is knowing that this free Gift of Grace from Our Father included a Measure of faith that was added to the faith Our Father placed in your inner spirit when you were born in your mother's womb.

Faith is knowing that Our Father gave you, as a born-again Christian, a Measure of Faith for two reasons. First of all, with your Measure of Faith, you learned that Our Father hates sin and how to separate your spirit being, your physical body, and the life you live from the sin Our Father hates. Secondly, through the Measure of Faith, you learned that when you became a born-again Christian, you became a part of your Lord's physical body on Planet Earth, His Church, while He is actually sitting at the right hand of Our Father in Heaven. Through the Measure of Faith, you learned that Our Father gave you some talents and abilities when you were born in your mother's womb, and some spiritual gifts in your Measure of Faith, so that you can fulfill the purpose in Your Lord's Church that He intends you to do. During the next few lessons, we are going to talk about how to put what you know about the Measure of Faith into believing or doing in your life.

I want to give you one illustration of the meaning of the word measure. When you became a Born-Again Christian, Our Father gave you a Measure of Faith, the amount you need to be the person in the Body of Christ that Our Father intends you to be. When my wife became a Born-Again Christian, Our Father gave her a Measure of Faith, a different measure than mine, so that she could be the person in the Body of Christ Our Father intends her to be. When my wife and I became husband and wife, we began a very important process in our lives: becoming spirit mates. Now, not only are we two spirits in the process of becoming one spirit, but our two Measures of Faith are in the process of becoming one Measure of Faith.

For example, Our Father has given me a gift for preaching and teaching His Word. Our Father has given my wife gifts. Our Father intends that the gift of preaching given to me in my Measure of Faith, and my wife's gift in her Measure of Faith, be blended together in one gift."

A LIVING SACRIFICE

One of the first things that happens when one receives a Measure of Faith is that he or she becomes a living sacrifice. Of course, being a living sacrifice is not dying like Your Lord did on the Cross or as some do in being a martyr. Being a living sacrifice is something one does while still living in one's physical body. To explain the meaning of living sacrifice, I will discuss some Scriptures. "After Our Father gave Patriarch Moses the Ten Commandments, He also gave Moses other laws that Our Father's Chosen people were to follow. Even before they arrived in the Promised Land, some of them were already worshipping the idol god named Molech. One of the laws Our Father gave was that His Chosen People should not sacrifice their children to Molech.

Leviticus 18:21
(King James Version)
21 And thou shalt not let any of thy seed pass through the fire to Molech, neither shalt thou profane the name of thy God: I am the Lord.

Leviticus 20:2
(King James Version)
2 Again, thou shalt say to the children of Israel, Whosoever he be of the children of Israel, or of the strangers that sojourn in Israel, that giveth any of his seed unto Molech; he shall surely be put to death: the people of the land shall stone him with stones.

The idol form of Molech was fairly tall and built so that a hot fire could burn inside it. The idol's arms were extended towards worshippers, with a fire beneath them, making the arms hot. Some of the worshippers of the idol would pass their children through the fire. That is, they would let their infant children be burned to some extent above extended arms or place them on the hot metal as a matter of purification and a sign of dedication to Molech. Some would even place an infant child on the arms of Molech and let the infant be a burning sacrifice. Such a worshipper of the idol Molech was alive when sacrificing a child to show one's dedication to the false god, but this type of action is not the meaning of a living sacrifice. You tell me what the difference is between this and abortion.

After Our Father had given Patriarch Abraham a miracle son from the seed of Abraham and the womb of Sarah, Our Father tested Abraham's obedience. Our Father told Abraham to take his miracle son, Isaac, and go to a mountain, build an altar, and sacrifice his son to Our Father like he would sacrifice a lamb. At that point in time, Abraham did not know of Our Father's law forbidding the sacrifice of a child, like some in neighboring territories were already sacrificing infants to Molech. Abraham prepared the altar, and his son was on the altar for the sacrifice. As he was raising his hand with the knife to make the sacrifice, an angel called to him and told him not to sacrifice his son, but rather he was to sacrifice a ram that was caught by his horns in the thicket.

Genesis 22:12-19
(King James Version)

12 And he said, Lay not thine hand upon the lad, neither do thou any thing unto him: for now I know that thou fearest God, seeing thou hast not withheld thy son, thine only son from me.
13 And Abraham lifted up his eyes, and looked, and behold behind him a ram caught in a thicket by his horns: and

Abraham went and took the ram, and offered him up for a burnt offering in the stead of his son.
14 And Abraham called the name of that place Jehovahjireh: as it is said to this day, In the mount of the Lord it shall be seen.
15 And the angel of the Lord called unto Abraham out of heaven the second time,
16 And said, By myself have I sworn, saith the Lord, for because thou hast done this thing, and hast not withheld thy son, thine only son:
17 That in blessing I will bless thee, and in multiplying I will multiply thy seed as the stars of the heaven, and as the sand which is upon the sea shore; and thy seed shall possess the gate of his enemies;
18 And in thy seed shall all the nations of the earth be blessed; because thou hast obeyed my voice.
19 So Abraham returned unto his young men, and they rose up and went together to Beersheba; and Abraham dwelt at Beersheba.

Part of this event is an illustration of a living sacrifice. Our Father was the most important person in Abraham's life, even more important than his son, Isaac. Our Father was so important to Abraham that he was willing to do anything Our Father told him, even sacrifice his son. A Born-Again Christian can be a living sacrifice when no person or anything is more important than Our Father. This is not the case in most believers' lives, and many don't realize it. This is why our father employs tests and trials to show them what their lives are like, as he did with Abraham. Here are three illustrations of being a living sacrifice. "It is difficult for some wives and some husbands to let Our Father be the most important person in their lives because one's mate becomes jealous when he or she makes Our Father the most important person in his or her life. "There are families who miss Church on Sunday nights and Wednesday nights because there are television programs they want to watch, or the parents decide their children have to go to bed early to rest for school the next day.

> When you became a Born-Again Christian, one of the main reasons that Our Father gave you a Measure of Faith is that you can be a living sacrifice by making Our Father the most important person in your life. This type of commitment, or the dedication of your life, is the beginning of your journey with your Measure of Faith.

* * *

Chapter 6: The Measure of Faith (Part 2)

One purpose of each Born Again Christian being given a Measure of Faith is to help that person do what is right. "When you were born in your mother's womb and Our Father created your spirit being in His image, He placed some of the qualities of His personality in you. Since Our Father is good, holy, and righteous, I trust that you also have these qualities within you. This is how the first man created by Our Father was when he was first placed in the Garden of Eden. Then Satan came into the picture. The qualities of the personality of Satan are opposite to those of Our Father – evil, unholy, and unrighteous, deceitful, immoral, and hateful. When Adam chose to disobey Our Father and obey Satan, Satan also placed the qualities of his personality in Adam. Thereafter, starting with Adam, whenever the seed of man results in a person being born in the womb of his or her mother, that person has both the qualities of Our Father's personality in him or her as well as the qualities of the personality of Satan.

Since the quality of hate has a stronger drive to force oneself on another person than love, when humans are left on their own without Divine help, the personality of Satan tends to dominate their lives. The personality of some animals is an example. They spend all their life trying to manipulate you into doing what they want done for them. This makes you make that animal a very self-centered being. This is what happens to humans if they are left alone with the qualities of the personality of Our Father and the personality of Satan: you become very self-centered and selfish. "This is why when you came to the Age of Choosing and became a Born-Again Christian, Our Father gave you a Measure of Faith. This is so that Holy Spirit can help you to overcome the qualities of the personality of Satan in your spirit and body.

Romans 5:12
(King James Version)
12 Wherefore, as by one man sin entered into the world, and death by sin; and so death passed upon all men, for that all have sinned:

Our Father is the father of the spirit part of your being. Adam is the father of the human part of your being. When Adam disobeyed Our Father, Satan placed sin or evil, including the personality qualities of Satan, within him. This sin lived in both the human and the spiritual parts of Adam. Then, when the seed of Adam was involved in a person being born in the womb of his wife, Eve, this sin was transferred to the person born in Eve's womb. Since then, every time a person is born in a mother's womb through the seed of a man, this sin is transferred to the person born in the mother's womb. This process is referred to as original sin or inherited sin. Through the Measure of Faith, a born-again Christian, with Holy Spirit assistance, can overcome the personality traits within one's being to manifest the personality traits of Our Father.

Matthew 15:15-20
(King James Version)
15 Then answered Peter and said unto him, Declare unto us this parable.
16 And Jesus said, Are ye also yet without understanding?
17 Do not ye yet understand, that whatsoever entereth in at the mouth goeth into the belly, and is cast out into the draught?
18 But those things which proceed out of the mouth come forth from the heart; and they defile the man.
19 For out of the heart proceed evil thoughts, murders, adulteries, fornications, thefts, false witness, blasphemies:
20 These are the things which defile a man: but to eat with unwashen hands defileth not a man.

PURSUING HOLINESS

In this passage of Scripture, some things are listed: personality qualities that can come from the original sin within a person. Through a Born-Again Christian's Measure of Faith Holy Spirit can help him or her in such a way that these things need not happen in his or her life. Human beings do not seem to have any problem giving their best efforts to accomplish things in life's natural and physical realms. Even some of you who are Born Again are willing to put forth your best efforts to accomplish natural and physical goals in life, but many do not channel the same enthusiasm and drive toward spiritual goals. This matter of subduing the personality traits of Satan within born-again Christians is not an easy matter. For all of Born-Again Christians, this is going to take the best spiritual effort you can put forth, and then you are going to have to sustain this effort as long as you are living in your human bodies. Then you will also discover that your personal efforts will not be enough, and that you will also need to receive some help from Holy Spirit through the Measure of Faith Our Father gave you when you became a born-again Christian.

Hebrews 12:12-17
(King James Version)
12 Wherefore lift up the hands which hang down, and the feeble knees;
13 And make straight paths for your feet, lest that which is lame be turned out of the way; but let it rather be healed.
14 Follow peace with all men, and holiness, without which no man shall see the Lord:
15 Looking diligently lest any man fail of the grace of God; lest any root of bitterness springing up trouble you, and thereby many be defiled;
16 Lest there be any fornicator, or profane person, as Esau, who for one morsel of meat sold his birthright.
17 For ye know how that afterward, when he would have inherited the blessing, he was rejected: for he found no place of repentance, though he sought it carefully with tears.

In these verses, Holy Spirit asks Born Again Christians to pursue holiness. This is how you overcome the personality traits of Satan within you. The context of this parable is that of a runner trying to win a race. The word pursue means that the runner is to put forth his or her best effort and run so fast and hard that he or she can no longer hold up his or her hands and arms properly, so one can breathe properly, and one's legs are so tired that he or she feels like he or she cannot take another step. In fact, if one does not spend enough time in training, that is, in personal daily worship and Bible study and worship on Sunday and at other times with other Born-Again Christians, one will not run a good race in subduing the personality traits of Satan. There is also a symbolic meaning to mention in this parable. The uplifted hands symbolize praise, and the bent knees symbolize prayer. One needs much praise and prayer to subdue the personality traits of Satan within oneself."

Ephesians 6:18
(King James Version)
18 Praying always with all prayer and supplication in the Spirit, and watching thereunto with all perseverance and supplication for all saints;

This putting forth of such a great effort to subdue the personality traits of Satan is not just a one-time event; it is a lifelong endeavor. Our Father gave you a Measure of Faith when you became a born-again Christian so that you can receive help as you continue to put forth your best spiritual effort to overcome the personality traits of Satan within you." "Our Father had all of the angels present when He engraved the Ten Commandments because of the importance of the commandments. He wanted them to understand the commandments so they could help us, Born Again Christians, to understand the importance of the commands.

OVERCOMING THE WORLD

As you know, according to Romans 12:1-2, you should not be conformed to this world because you received a Measure of Faith when you became a born-again Christian. Keep in mind that the definition of the word world is the universe and those who are opposed to Our

Father. Since Satan is the chief one opposed to Our Father, he is always trying to get you, even as a Born-Again Christian, to do things his way rather than Our Father's way. Thus, conforming to the world is about doing things Satan's way. The Ten Commandments are very important in preventing this from happening. "As I have explained before, there are three types of laws Our Father created for you living on Planet Earth. There are the natural laws of the universe and Planet Earth. There are the physical laws for "Your human body- And there are the Ten Commandments and other spiritual laws for you as a spirit being living in your physical body. Our Father's plan is that you use the Ten Commandments as the guideline for applying not only the Ten Commandments and other spiritual laws to your life, but also the natural and physical laws. That Measure of Faith. What you received when you became a Born-Again Christian can enable you to follow the Ten Commandments in such a way that you will not do the ways of Satan in your life."

Matthew 22:34-40
(King James Version)
34 But when the Pharisees had heard that he had put the Sadducees to silence, they were gathered together.
35 Then one of them, which was a lawyer, asked him a question, tempting him, and saying,
36 Master, which is the great commandment in the law?
37 Jesus said unto him, Thou shalt love the Lord thy God with all thy heart, and with all thy soul, and with all thy mind.
38 This is the first and great commandment.
39 And the second is like unto it, Thou shalt love thy neighbour as thyself.
40 On these two commandments hang all the law and the

prophets.

The Ten Commandments can be summarized as Jesus did in the first and second commandments. The first five commandments of the Ten Commandments concern worshipping Our Father, including honoring father and mother as part of that worship. The second five commandments are about proper relationships with your neighbor. Christ says that all spiritual laws are based on the Ten Commandments.

Galatians 5:16-26
(King James Version)
16 This I say then, Walk in the Spirit, and ye shall not fulfil
the lust of the flesh.
17 For the flesh lusteth against the Spirit, and the Spirit
against the flesh: and these are contrary the one to the
other: so that ye cannot do the things that ye would.
18 But if ye be led of the Spirit, ye are not under the law.
19 Now the works of the flesh are manifest, which are these;
Adultery, fornication, uncleanness, lasciviousness,
20 Idolatry, witchcraft, hatred, variance, emulations,
wrath, strife, seditions, heresies,
21 Envyings, murders, drunkenness, revellings, and such
like: of the which I tell you before, as I have also told you in
time past, that they which do such things shall not inherit
the kingdom of God.
22 But the fruit of the Spirit is love, joy, peace,
longsuffering, gentleness, goodness, faith,
23 Meekness, temperance: against such there is no law.
24 And they that are Christ's have crucified the flesh with

the affections and lusts.
25 If we live in the Spirit, let us also walk in the Spirit.
26 Let us not be desirous of vain glory, provoking one another, envying one another.

HOLY SPIRIT AND YOU

The works of the flesh will happen if you do not obey the Ten Commandments. The fruit of the spirit will happen when, through your Measure of Faith, you let Holy Spirit help you keep the Ten Commandments."

Matthew 5:3-12
(King James Version)
3 Blessed are the poor in spirit: for theirs is the kingdom of heaven.
4 Blessed are they that mourn: for they shall be comforted.
5 Blessed are the meek: for they shall inherit the earth.
6 Blessed are they which do hunger and thirst after righteousness: for they shall be filled.
7 Blessed are the merciful: for they shall obtain mercy.
8 Blessed are the pure in heart: for they shall see God.
9 Blessed are the peacemakers: for they shall be called the children of God.
10 Blessed are they which are persecuted for righteousness' sake: for theirs is the kingdom of heaven.
11 Blessed are ye, when men shall revile you, and persecute you, and shall say all manner of evil against you falsely, for my sake.
12 Rejoice, and be exceeding glad: for great is your reward in heaven: for so persecuted they the prophets which were

before you.

Only those born-again Christians who are keeping the Ten Commandments can receive these nine blessings of The Beatitudes." Question: "How do the natural laws of time our Father created affect your life?" "Does this involve any daily decision-making for you?" "Do the physical laws that Our Father has created for your physical body have any daily decisions that need to be made?"

In Romans 12:1-2, Holy Spirit had Apostle Paul write that one of the things Born-Again Christians are to do with the Measure of Faith they acquired when they received Our Father's Grace is to renew their minds. The word for mind refers not only to intellectual activity but also to a sense of moral values. This idea is about Christians making daily decisions to apply the meaning of the Ten Commandments to their lives. "One of the challenges for you, Born Again Christians, is to start to become holy as Our Father is holy. The Ten Commandments that Our Father engraved on two tablets of stone and gave to Patriarch Moses are the basis of your holiness. This is not. A matter of trying to adapt these spiritual laws of Our Father to your lives, as some are trying to do. This is about recognizing that these spiritual laws are eternal; they do not change. Your Measure of Faith includes the ability to make daily decisions as to how to adapt the events of your life to the teachings of the Ten Commandments. Therefore, each day as you scan your life and activities, ask yourself what you must do. You make sure they do not interfere with any of the ten commandments and then ask God how you would carry out your activities of the day.

Romans 7:12
(King James Version)
12 Wherefore the law is holy, and the commandment holy,

and just, and good.

There is a lesson to learn from this verse about becoming holy. When you came to the Age of Choosing and chose to become a Born-Again Christian, you began to realize that you had both personality traits of Our Father and personality traits of Satan within you. In fact, you have about an equal amount of personality traits from both. The laws of our Father, the Ten Commandments, are holy. When you keep renewing daily the meaning of the Ten Commandments, you are receiving these laws of Our Father through your mind into your inner being. Because these laws of Our Father are holy, this means that you now have more holiness, and the personality traits of Our Father are now more than those of Satan. If you were to begin to disobey one of the commandments, the opposite would happen, and you would end up with more personality traits of Satan than of Our Father." The Quality of Faith that Our Father placed in you when you were born in your mother's womb is the faith that helps you exist in the natural world, that is, Planet Earth. The Measure of Faith that you received when you accepted Our Father's gift of grace to you when you became a Born-Again Christian, is for the purpose of helping you to be the part of the Body of Christ that you were created to be."

You have been told that one of the reasons for the Measure of Faith you received when you became a Born Again Christian is so that Christ Your Lord can place you in His Body, His Church, where He wants you, and give you the necessary gifts to do the purpose for which Our Father created you. There is one teaching of your society today that greatly hinders this concept. The idea taught is that each of you is responsible for your destiny or purpose in life. You are being. encouraged to do your own thing to find meaning in life. Thus, our society evaluates some people to be greater than others. "There are no generals or giants in the Body of Christ, Your Lord. There is an equality of importance of each believer in Christ's Church; thus, if any would be a general or giant, all are generals and giants. One of the present-day problems in Christ's Body, His Church, is the problem of control. This problem was present even in Old Testament times. For example, after King Ahab took Jezebel as his wife, this queen tried to destroy the prophets of Our Father, including Prophet Elijah, as a way of encouraging Our Father's Chosen People to worship Baal. (See 1 Kings 18:4, 13, 19:1-3.) Apostle John also mentioned the problem of some laypeople trying to control the prophets or pastors of Churches. (See Revelation 2:20.) The Temple worship of Our Father's Chosen People is Biblically listed as the Old Testament Church. (See Acts 7:38.) The leaders of the Old Testament Church were responsible for the stoning of Deacon Stephen. (See Acts 6:15, 7:59.) In the present day, sometimes the lay people try to control the pastor, and sometimes the pastor controls the lay people.

As you know, there is one head of the Church, Christ Your Lord. (See Colossians 1:17-18; Ephesians 5:23-24.) Christ, the head of His Church, places each of you, born-again Christians, in His Body as it pleases Him. (1 Corinthians 12:18.) This means that as Born-Again Christians in the Body of Christ, all of you are under the authority of Christ, and none are under the authority of each other.

THE YOKE OF HUMILITY

Matthew 11:28-30
(King James Version)
28 Come unto me, all ye that labour and are heavy laden,
and I will give you rest.
29 Take my yoke upon you, and learn of me; for I am meek

and lowly in heart: and ye shall find rest unto your souls. 30 For my yoke is easy, and my burden is light.

In this parable, the yoke is your keeping of the Ten Commandments. The wooden yoke was for a team of oxen. The head of one ox was placed through one side of the yoke, and the head of another ox was placed through the other side. Then the yoke was connected to a load, so that as the two oxen pushed against the Yoke with equal force, the load moved. As Born-Again Christians, through the Measures of Faith you have, you are to be yoked together to do things for Christ. Each Born Again Christian with his or her gifts as needed, and the ministry of each one is equally important." (See 1 Corinthians 12:18-27.)

Ephesians 4:16
(King James Version)
16 From whom the whole body fitly joined together and compacted by that which every joint supplieth, according to the effectual working in the measure of every part, maketh increase of the body unto the edifying of itself in love.

Note again that according to Romans 12:1-3, when you receive your Measure of Faith when you are Born Again, a quality of humility comes with the Measure of Faith, when you become adopted children of Our Father. This entitles you to many rights and privileges. The greatest of these rights and privileges is your coming future life in Heaven, and Our Father will never ask you to give this up. But there are many of these rights and privileges that you have a right to enjoy while you are living on Planet Earth. Since you are created in the image of Our Father, you have a quality of humility within you that has the potential for you to make these rights and privileges secondary in your lives and make the primary factor in your lives that of becoming servants to the needs of others. Your Measure of Faith can enable you to do this."

Philippians 2:5-11
(King James Version)
5 Let this mind be in you, which was also in Christ Jesus:
6 Who, being in the form of God, thought it not robbery to be equal with God:
7 But made himself of no reputation, and took upon him the form of a servant, and was made in the likeness of men:
8 And being found in fashion as a man, he humbled himself, and became obedient unto death, even the death of the cross.
9 Wherefore God also hath highly exalted him, and given him a name which is above every name:
10 That at the name of Jesus every knee should bow, of things in heaven, and things in earth, and things under the earth;
11 And that every tongue should confess that Jesus Christ is Lord, to the glory of God the Father.

Since Our Father, Christ, and Holy Spirit are equal persons in the one person of the Godhead, Christ had every right to be at the right hand of Our Father in Heaven. This quality of humility can be seen in that Your Lord chose to give up that right, and lower Himself and come down to Planet Earth, become obedient to the will of Our Father, and die on a cross as He became a servant of your needs. This is the type of humility that Our Father desires for His Children to have, as they become parts of the Body of Christ.

Thus, your Measure of Faith can enable you to become more concerned about helping others with their needs than you are in receiving from Our Father what is rightfully yours.

* * *

IV

IV. Living In Two Worlds

liv·ing
/ˈliviNG/

the pursuit of a lifestyle of the specified type.

world
/wərld/

a planet or dimension together with all of its countries, peoples, and natural features.

Chapter 7: Living in Two Worlds

After I was born again at my father's church, I did not realize at the time that I had begun to live in two worlds. Don't get me wrong, I was alive and breathing, but I was spiritually dead, and my physical body was breathing. I did not realize I was truly alive till years later. The spiritual Kingdom of our Father is like the wind blowing; you cannot actually see the wind blowing with your physical eyes, but you can be aware of the presence of the wind blowing.

So let me say it again, but a little differently, when I confessed and repented of my sins, Christ moved into my spirit being. (Rev. 3:20) When Christ fulfilled the prophecy of John the Baptist and baptized me with Holy Spirit, Matthew 3:1. The presence of Christ living within me returned to the right hand of our Father in heaven (1 Peter 3:22), and Holy Spirit moved within me, my spirit being. My spirit, being living in my physical body, became the temple or dwelling place of Holy Spirit. (1Cor. 3:16) Therefore, Holy Spirit is in the spiritual kingdom of Our Father around me. My Guardian Angels are also living in the spiritual kingdom around me, combating Satan and demons that are in the spiritual realm around me. Eventually, all those of us who become Born-Again Christians while living on Earth will be spirit beings living in Heaven, and those of us who do not become Born-Again Christians will be spirit beings living in Hell. "One of the important reasons Our Father gave you a Measure of Faith when you became a Born-Again Christian is so that you can have communication with the Godhead living within you, around you, and in Heaven. Those who are not born-again Christians do not have a Measure of Faith for this communication."

Luke 17:20-21
(King James Version)
20 And when he was demanded of the Pharisees, when the kingdom of God should come, he answered them and said, The kingdom of God cometh not with observation:
21 Neither shall they say, Lo here! or, lo there! for, behold, the kingdom of God is within you.

THE MAIN PURPOSE OF FAITH

There are a few exceptions, but generally speaking, the spiritual kingdom of Our Father is not experienced by your five senses created to sense the natural and physical world around you: sight, touch, hearing, taste, and smell."

Colossians 1:15-16
(King James Version)
15 Who is the image of the invisible God, the firstborn of every creature:
16 For by him were all things created, that are in heaven,

and that are in earth, visible and invisible, whether they be thrones, or dominions, or principalities, or powers: all things were created by him, and for him:

```
The invisible refers to the spirit realm co-existing with
the natural world, including Holy Spirit living in your
spirit being, you as a spirit being, the angels and demons
living in the spirit realm around you, and the spirit places
of Heaven and Hell and the spirit beings in Heaven and Hell.
```

Hebrews 11:1
(King James Version)
11 Now faith is the substance of things hoped for, the evidence of things not seen.

The Measure of Faith in born-again Christians is the evidence or proof that there is a spirit realm and our means of communication with the Godhead of the spirit realm. This will be your basic communication with them as long as you are living in your physical body. If you had conversations with the angels on a regular basis, that is not the way you would converse with the Godhead. If you were able to communicate with angels, it would not be because of the Measure of | Faith you received when you became a Born-Again Christian. There are two reasons that you could communicate with them. Our Father would have to open your eyes so you can see them as a light form being. Secondly, they would have to come to you, and then you could have conversations similar to those you have with other human beings. The Measure of Faith you have been given is only for communication with the Godhead, who is invisible to your natural eyes. Here are some scriptures that support our communication with the Godhead.

In Matthew 6:6, your Lord instructed you to go into the privacy of your prayer closet and pray to our Father. Secondly, the teaching of Your Lord recorded in John 14:12-14 means that even though Your Lord is seated at the right hand of Our Father in Heaven, you can pray to Him. Also in Acts 5:3, it is recorded that Ananias told a lie to Holy Spirit. This means that Ananias had a conversation or a time of prayer with Holy Spirit. Then also note that in Acts 5:4, it is stated that when Ananias told a lie to (HS), he also was telling a lie to Our Father.

When you pray, you can either direct your prayer to Our Father in Heaven, to Your Lord sitting at the right hand of Our Father in Heaven, or to Holy Spirit living within you as a spirit being in your physical body, or to Holy Spirit living around you. Because of your Measure of Faith, whoever of them you pray to, the exchange of communication takes place between you and Holy Spirit in your inner spirit. Then Holy Spirit communicates your prayers to Your Lord at the right hand of Our Father, and He communicates your prayer to Our Father. When Our Father communicates a response to you, He tells Christ, Christ tells Holy Spirit, and Holy Spirit tells you. I used to wonder about this when I was a young believer, and you may not think this type of semantics is necessary, given that it's God. However, you must remember that there are laws that govern that world, just as there are in this one.

One other important matter in this communication through your Measure of Faith is that you can initiate a communication to Our Father any time you desire. Even though Our Father/Christ/Holy Spirit is invisible to your physical eyes, every time you speak a word of communication to Our Father/Christ/Holy Spirit. Holy Spirit hears it and communicates it to Your Lord at the right hand of Our Father in Heaven, and He communicates it to Our Father. You cannot have this kind of conversation with any other being in the spirit realm, either on Planet Earth or in Heaven.

MANIFESTATIONS VS APPEARANCE

The reason I'm addressing this is that in the last days, we will see many weird things, specifically people supposedly returning from the dead and communicating with others. As well as ET's landing and making contact, which is not ET's but fallen Angels.

2 Corinthians 5:8
(King James Version)
8 We are confident, I say, and willing rather to be absent from the body, and to be present with the Lord.

This means that when a Born-Again Christian experiences physical death, he or she goes to Heaven. Now, I want to explain why Our Father would not send a saint in Heaven back to Planet Earth, as He does with a Messenger and a guardian angel.

Angels have the ability to defeat demons, as demonstrated when they defeated Satan and the rebellious angels in Heaven. While we, Born Again Christians, are living on Earth, there are two ways that your Measure of Faith enables you to defeat Satan and demons. 1) When Satan tries to influence you to do something. You can resist or refuse to do what Satan wants you to do. (See James 4:7.) You can even quote Scripture like your Lord did when Satan tempted Him. When you resist Satan, your Measure of Faith permits Holy Spirit to strengthen you. When you resist Satan in this manner, he will flee from you. 2) You can take the offensive against Satan and command him in the

Name of Jesus. (See Acts 16:18.) When you do this, you are actually praying a prayer through your Measure of Faith that enables the angels and Holy Spirit to attack Satan.

One who became a saint in Heaven was formerly living on Earth. Holy Spirit is within and around that one. When that Born Again Christian goes to Heaven, Holy Spirit does not go with them. So, if Our Father would send a saint in Heaven back to Planet Earth as a messenger, that saint, without Holy Spirit assistance, would not have any way to confront Satan and demons. Our Father does not endanger any saint by sending the saint to Planet Earth as a messenger. Therefore, if you ever think you hear the voice of a loved one living in Heaven, or see such a loved one near you, that would actually be a manifestation of an angel. There are times when Our Father will use such an angel manifestation to get the attention of a born-again Christian.

Hebrews 11:39
(King James Version)
39 And these all, having obtained a good report through faith, received not the promise:

Hebrews 12:9
(King James Version)
9 Furthermore we have had fathers of our flesh which corrected us, and we gave them reverence: shall we not much rather be in subjection unto the Father of spirits, and live?

This Scripture provides a description and location of the Born-Again Christians who have departed from Planet Earth in the experience of physical death. They are living in Heaven and observing the activities of Born-Again Christians on Planet Earth. They only witness pleasant things happening on Planet Earth, as there are no tears and sadness in Heaven. The Born-Again Christians in Heaven are citizens of Heaven, no longer sojourners on Planet Earth.

Genesis 18:1-15
(King James Version)

18 And the Lord appeared unto him in the plains of Mamre: and he sat in the tent door in the heat of the day;
2 And he lift up his eyes and looked, and, lo, three men stood by him: and when he saw them, he ran to meet them from the tent door, and bowed himself toward the ground,
3 And said, My Lord, if now I have found favour in thy sight, pass not away, I pray thee, from thy servant:
4 Let a little water, I pray you, be fetched, and wash your feet, and rest yourselves under the tree:
5 And I will fetch a morsel of bread, and comfort ye your hearts; after that ye shall pass on: for therefore are ye come to your servant. And they said, So do, as thou hast said.
6 And Abraham hastened into the tent unto Sarah, and said, Make ready quickly three measures of fine meal, knead it, and make cakes upon the hearth.
7 And Abraham ran unto the herd, and fetcht a calf tender and good, and gave it unto a young man; and he hasted to dress it.
8 And he took butter, and milk, and the calf which he had dressed, and set it before them; and he stood by them under

the tree, and they did eat.
9 And they said unto him, Where is Sarah thy wife? And he said, Behold, in the tent.
10 And he said, I will certainly return unto thee according to the time of life; and, lo, Sarah thy wife shall have a son. And Sarah heard it in the tent door, which was behind him.
11 Now Abraham and Sarah were old and well stricken in age; and it ceased to be with Sarah after the manner of women.
12 Therefore Sarah laughed within herself, saying, After I am waxed old shall I have pleasure, my lord being old also?
13 And the Lord said unto Abraham, Wherefore did Sarah laugh, saying, Shall I of a surety bear a child, which am old?
14 Is any thing too hard for the Lord? At the time appointed I will return unto thee, according to the time of life, and Sarah shall have a son.
15 Then Sarah denied, saying, I laughed not; for she was afraid. And he said, Nay; but thou didst laugh.

Hebrews 13:2
(King James Version)
2 Be not forgetful to entertain strangers: for thereby some have entertained angels unawares.

Abraham saw three angels manifesting themselves as men on Earth. These types of angel manifestations still seem very real to those who experience them.

WITCHES AND MEDIUMS

So why did I go down this road, you may say, Pastor? For two reasons: in these last days, as I said, there will be an increase in witches and mediums in the church, and also to show you how your measure of faith operates. It can't call someone from heaven to earth.

1 Samuel 28:3-25
(King James Version)
3 Now Samuel was dead, and all Israel had lamented him, and buried him in Ramah, even in his own city. And Saul had put away those that had familiar spirits, and the wizards, out of the land.
4 And the Philistines gathered themselves together, and came and pitched in Shunem: and Saul gathered all Israel together, and they pitched in Gilboa.
5 And when Saul saw the host of the Philistines, he was afraid, and his heart greatly trembled.
6 And when Saul enquired of the Lord, the Lord answered him not, neither by dreams, nor by Urim, nor by prophets.
7 Then said Saul unto his servants, Seek me a woman that hath a familiar spirit, that I may go to her, and enquire of her. And his servants said to him, Behold, there is a woman that hath a familiar spirit at Endor.
8 And Saul disguised himself, and put on other raiment, and he went, and two men with him, and they came to the woman by night: and he said, I pray thee, divine unto me by the familiar spirit, and bring me him up, whom I shall name unto thee.
9 And the woman said unto him, Behold, thou knowest what Saul hath done, how he hath cut off those that have

familiar spirits, and the wizards, out of the land: wherefore then layest thou a snare for my life, to cause me to die?
10 And Saul sware to her by the Lord, saying, As the Lord liveth, there shall no punishment happen to thee for this thing.
11 Then said the woman, Whom shall I bring up unto thee? And he said, Bring me up Samuel.
12 And when the woman saw Samuel, she cried with a loud voice: and the woman spake to Saul, saying, Why hast thou deceived me? for thou art Saul.
13 And the king said unto her, Be not afraid: for what sawest thou? And the woman said unto Saul, I saw gods ascending out of the earth.
14 And he said unto her, What form is he of? And she said, An old man cometh up; and he is covered with a mantle. And Saul perceived that it was Samuel, and he stooped with his face to the ground, and bowed himself.
15 And Samuel said to Saul, Why hast thou disquieted me, to bring me up? And Saul answered, I am sore distressed; for the Philistines make war against me, and God is departed from me, and answereth me no more, neither by prophets, nor by dreams: therefore I have called thee, that thou mayest make known unto me what I shall do.
16 Then said Samuel, Wherefore then dost thou ask of me, seeing the Lord is departed from thee, and is become thine enemy?
17 And the Lord hath done to him, as he spake by me: for the Lord hath rent the kingdom out of thine hand, and given it to thy neighbour, even to David:
18 Because thou obeyedst not the voice of the Lord, nor executedst his fierce wrath upon Amalek, therefore hath the

Lord done this thing unto thee this day.
19 Moreover the Lord will also deliver Israel with thee into
the hand of the Philistines: and to morrow shalt thou and
thy sons be with me: the Lord also shall deliver the host of
Israel into the hand of the Philistines.
20 Then Saul fell straightway all along on the earth, and
was sore afraid, because of the words of Samuel: and there
was no strength in him; for he had eaten no bread all the
day, nor all the night.
21 And the woman came unto Saul, and saw that he was
sore troubled, and said unto him, Behold, thine handmaid
hath obeyed thy voice, and I have put my life in my hand,
and have hearkened unto thy words which thou spakest
unto me.
22 Now therefore, I pray thee, hearken thou also unto the
voice of thine handmaid, and let me set a morsel of bread
before thee; and eat, that thou mayest have strength, when
thou goest on thy way.
23 But he refused, and said, I will not eat. But his servants,
together with the woman, compelled him; and he hearkened
unto their voice. So he arose from the earth, and sat upon
the bed.
24 And the woman had a fat calf in the house; and she
hasted, and killed it, and took flour, and kneaded it, and did
bake unleavened bread thereof:
25 And she brought it before Saul, and before his servants;
and they did eat. Then they rose up, and went away that
night.

The Philistines were gathering to attack the nation of Our Father's Chosen People. Usually, in times like that, King Saul would ask Prophet

Samuel for advice on what to do. Prophet Samuel had died, so King Saul tried to get an answer from Our Father. Since the spirit of the Lord had left King Saul, he received no answer. So, King Saul, in a deceptive way, asked the witch or medium of En Dor to call forth the spirit of Prophet Samuel, who was dead. The medium was able to call forth the spirit of the Prophet Samuel, or at least King Saul thought the medium had succeeded in doing so. (See 1 Samuel 28:14.)"

There is one important thing to note about what the medium accomplished for King Saul. The image she called forth lacked any glow. If this had been Prophet Samuel, who was living in the presence of Our Father in Paradise, he would have had a glow about him. The spirit of the Lord was no longer with King Saul, so Our Father was not involved in this experience. What came forth that day was a demon manifesting itself as Prophet Samuel. Sometimes the demon manifestations that come through a medium, channel, spirit guide, or séance appear to be a positive, helpful message. There is one important thing to remember about any guidance received from Satan. At first, the guidance will always bring pleasure to you, but sooner or later, Satan will always add hurt and pain to what he is doing in one's life. Our Father sends a saint living in Heaven to a person on Planet Earth, but only in a vision or dream, never through a medium, channel, spirit guide, or séance. Your Measure of Faith functions with visions and dreams, but not with mediums, channel guides, spirit guides, and séances."

Exodus 34:29-30
(King James Version)
29 And it came to pass, when Moses came down from mount
Sinai with the two tables of testimony in Moses' hand,
when he came down from the mount, that Moses wist not
that the skin of his face shone while he talked with him.

30 And when Aaron and all the children of Israel saw Moses, behold, the skin of his face shone; and they were afraid to come nigh him.

```
When Patriarch Moses came down from the mountain after being
in the presence of Our Father for forty days, he had a glow
to his face. The saints in Heaven have a glow on their faces
because they are in the presence of Our Father.
```

THE GLORY OF HIS PRESENCE

In Acts 12:5-11, when the Apostle Peter first saw the angel, he looked so much like Moses and Elijah that he thought he was seeing another vision. It was not until they were out of prison and walking down the street that he finally realized he was not having a vision but a real experience. After Apostle Peter realized he was not having a vision, Our Father took away his ability to see him, and even though he could not see him again and thought he was leaving, he stayed with him."

When Your Lord and Apostles Peter, James, and John were coming down out of the mountain after the experience, Your Lord told them that they should not tell the vision they had seen until after the Resurrection of Your Lord. (See Matthew 17:9.) The change that the apostles saw in Your Lord was not a vision; that was a real change in Your Lord. The vision that the apostles saw was the appearance of Patriarch Moses and Prophet Elijah. Our Father sent them to the top of the mountain through a vision, and they were glistening white because they had come from the Heavenly Glory Presence of Our Father. (They were not angels manifesting as them; had it been they would not have been glowing) "Finally, it should be noted that Our

Father often gives these visions as a person is worshipping privately or gathered together with a group of Born-Again Christians. For example, when Apostle John had his vision of the Lord and all that he saw in the Book of Revelation, he was worshipping on the Lord's Day. (See Revelation 1:10.) Visions and dreams are two of the ways Our Father uses the Measure of Faith in Born Again Christians to let you see some of the invisible spirit realm. Most often, Our Father will use an angel manifestation of a saint in Heaven that a worshipper would recognize to minister to the worshipper. But there are a few times when Our Father sends a saint from Heaven in a dream or vision of the worshipper."

2 Corinthians 12:1-6
(King James Version)
12 It is not expedient for me doubtless to glory. I will come to visions and revelations of the Lord.
2 I knew a man in Christ above fourteen years ago, (whether in the body, I cannot tell; or whether out of the body, I cannot tell: God knoweth;) such an one caught up to the third heaven.
3 And I knew such a man, (whether in the body, or out of the body, I cannot tell: God knoweth;)
4 How that he was caught up into paradise, and heard unspeakable words, which it is not lawful for a man to utter.
5 Of such an one will I glory: yet of myself I will not glory, but in mine infirmities.
6 For though I would desire to glory, I shall not be a fool; for I will say the truth: but now I forbear, lest any man should think of me above that which he seeth me to be, or that he heareth of me.

As Apostle Paul was writing this letter to the Christians at Corinth, Holy Spirit had him include the experience of one of his visions. There is an important difference to note between this vision of Apostle Paul and the vision of Apostle John that he had him record for the Book of Revelation. In Apostle John's vision, the voice he heard and what he saw came down from Heaven to him. (See Revelation 1:10.) In the vision of Apostle Paul, he was caught up in the Heavenly Presence of Our Father. (See 2 Corinthians 12:3-4.) This is important to note as there are a few times when a Born-Again Christian is taken up into Heaven to see some of the invisible spirit realm."

I'm only talking about visions now, a person leaving their body and walking around in heaven is something different.

* * *

Chapter 8: Living In Two Worlds (Part 2)

Romans 8:26
(King James Version)
26 Likewise the Spirit also helpeth our infirmities: for we know not what we should pray for as we ought: but the Spirit itself maketh intercession for us with groanings which cannot be uttered.

When you pray a prayer either to Our Father, Your Lord, or to Holy Spirit, he is the One who hears your prayer because he is living in your inner spirit. During those times, you prayed when you had some questions, he always heard your prayers, and then he prayed the appropriate prayer to Our Father. In our text verse, it is about born-again Christians praying when they have weaknesses or infirmities. A weakness is a lack of understanding of the natural world and the spirit realm around one, so that one cannot pray for the correct or best answer or solution to a problem or illness. When Holy Spirit relays these prayers to Our Father, he knows the correct or best answer, so that is what he relays to Our Father. There are times when the burden of the problem or illness is so great and one's understanding of the problem is so insufficient that all one can do is to groan in one's inner spirit. Of course, different levels of groanings can lead to travail. During those times, Holy Spirit interprets one's groans when he relays the prayer to Our Father. There are times when one is so impressed with the glory of Our Father that he or she can only sit, kneel, stand, or lie in silence. In those times of worship, Holy Spirit expresses the reverence and appreciation of that person to Our Father. Finally, Pentecostal Christians have an important understanding. You know that when you do not know how to pray, if you pray in your prayer language of tongues, Holy Spirit will pray the appropriate prayer to Our Father.

Matthew 6:8
(King James Version)
8 Be not ye therefore like unto them: for your Father knoweth what things ye have need of, before ye ask him.

Since Our Father knows of your needs even before you pray, you do not pray to inform Our Father of your needs. The purpose of your praying is to enable Holy Spirit to help you apply your Measure of Faith to your needs. (Where is your confidence? How much of the word is bearing fruit within you? As far as communication is concerned, continue to remember that your Measure of Faith is only for communication with Our Father, plus I will say it again, you can grow your measure to appropriate levels to declare and degree your needs."

DIFFERENT WAYS OF SEEING

Your measure of faith also helps you see what our Father wants you to see; remember, there are different levels of seeing. The basics that all believers begin with are the eyes of their hearts being enlightened, as Paul said. Of course, this is Holy Spirit placing thoughts in your mind from the communication he has received from the Godhead. Then there are gifts one is given to see into the spirit realm around them by angels coming to them, or one may also see in a vision form. Just as the woman who wrote "Blessed Assurance" was blind, she wrote about seeing the angels ascending and descending. She did not see them with her physical eyes but with the eyes of her spirit. I mentioned this because we want to examine some verses that speak about things that can cause blindness in one's spiritual eyes, even with the measure of faith.

Matthew 23:25-28
(King James Version)
25 Woe unto you, scribes and Pharisees, hypocrites! for ye make clean the outside of the cup and of the platter, but within they are full of extortion and excess.
26 Thou blind Pharisee, cleanse first that which is within the cup and platter, that the outside of them may be clean also.
27 Woe unto you, scribes and Pharisees, hypocrites! for ye are like unto whited sepulchres, which indeed appear beautiful outward, but are within full of dead men's bones, and of all uncleanness.
28 Even so ye also outwardly appear righteous unto men, but within ye are full of hypocrisy and iniquity.

DON'T BECOME SPIRITUALLY BLINDED

It is evident that the Pharisees exhibited a form of dishonesty, as their outward lives appeared righteous, but their inward spirits were not. One of the things that happened was that they were filling their cups (what they drank) and their platters (what they ate) dishonestly. Not only was this true for the Pharisees, but it is also true for some Born Again Christians. When dishonesty continues, it will always make a person spiritually blind."

Romans 2:17-24
(King James Version)
17 Behold, thou art called a Jew, and restest in the law, and makest thy boast of God,
18 And knowest his will, and approvest the things that are more excellent, being instructed out of the law;
19 And art confident that thou thyself art a guide of the blind, a light of them which are in darkness,
20 An instructor of the foolish, a teacher of babes, which hast the form of knowledge and of the truth in the law.
21 Thou therefore which teachest another, teachest thou not thyself? thou that preachest a man should not steal, dost thou steal?
22 Thou that sayest a man should not commit adultery, dost thou commit adultery? thou that abhorrest idols, dost thou commit sacrilege?
23 Thou that makest thy boast of the law, through breaking the law dishonourest thou God?
24 For the name of God is blasphemed among the Gentiles through you, as it is written.

In verse 19, Holy Spirit states that a person who does not know the truth of Our Father's Word is blind. When one hears the Word of Our Father, one sees the light and is no longer blind. Now note this. If one teaches a truth that he or she is not living in his or her life, that one will become blind in his or her spiritual eyes, even though he or she teaches the truth of Our Father's Word.

2 Peter 1:5-9
(King James Version)
5 And beside this, giving all diligence, add to your faith virtue; and to virtue knowledge;
6 And to knowledge temperance; and to temperance patience; and to patience godliness;
7 And to godliness brotherly kindness; and to brotherly kindness charity.
8 For if these things be in you, and abound, they make you that ye shall neither be barren nor unfruitful in the knowledge of our Lord Jesus Christ.
9 But he that lacketh these things is blind, and cannot see afar off, and hath forgotten that he was purged from his old sins.

After a person becomes a born-again Christian and receives a Measure of Faith from our Father, one should add the qualities of virtue, knowledge, self-control, perseverance, godliness, brotherly kindness, and love to one's life. If a Born-Again Christian does not continue to grow and mature in one's Christian life, one's spiritual eyes will become blind." That means one not only impairs one's ability to hear the truth but also is not able to hear the thoughts of Holy Spirit.

Revelation 3:17

(King James Version)
17 Because thou sayest, I am rich, and increased with goods, and have need of nothing; and knowest not that thou art wretched, and miserable, and poor, and blind, and naked:

```
If a Born-Again Christian begins to measure one's spiritual
life by how prosperous one is, that is, how many worldly
goods one has, that one is beginning to become spiritually
blind.
```

Matthew 7:3
(King James Version)
3 And why beholdest thou the mote that is in thy brother's eye, but considerest not the beam that is in thine own eye?

First of all, three big logs are pride (arrogance), jealousy, and covetousness. Secondly, if you begin to see the faults and weaknesses in the lives of other people more than you see your own faults and weaknesses, you will be in the process of becoming spiritually blind. Most of the understanding that Born Again Christians have of the invisible spirit realm around them comes through their spirit eyes as they communicate with Holy Spirit through their Measure of Faith. When one's spiritual eyes become blind, one cannot see or receive any understanding of the invisible spirit realm. In the same way, if you lose your eyesight, you cannot perceive things around you, thereby finding it hard to understand what things you are hearing. Not seeing in the spirit realm is not about being unable to literally see, but rather about being unable to understand what you hear and see. That also includes Holy Spirit.

COMMUNICATING WITH THE INVISIBLE GOD

In a very real sense, the Bible is a group of letters from the Invisible One, Our Father, to Born Again Christians. When you read these letters, you learn much about the Person of Our Father/Christ/Holy Spirit. So, one very important way for Born Again Christians to see and understand Our Father, who is invisible, is to read, study, and meditate upon the Scriptures. The Measure of Faith Our Father gave to each Born Again Christian enables you to see the invisible Our Father/Christ/Holy Spirit with your spirit eyes as you read the Bible."

Romans 4:3
(King James Version)
3 For what saith the scripture? Abraham believed God, and it was counted unto him for righteousness.
From reading the word, we have learned much about his character and life, even though he is totally invisible to us.

2 Timothy 3:16
(King James Version)
16 All scripture is given by inspiration of God, and is profitable for doctrine, for reproof, for correction, for instruction in righteousness:

2 Peter 1:21
(King James Version)
21 For the prophecy came not in old time by the will of man: but holy men of God spake as they were moved by the Holy Ghost.

Not only did Holy Spirit inspire people to write what eventually became part of the Bible, but he also inspires those who read the Bible. The word inspired means to breathe upon. As Our Father breathed His life into the first man, Adam, so through Holy Spirit. Our Father breathed His life into the Scriptures. Thus, when a Born-Again Christian, with his or her Measure of Faith, reads the Bible, that one sees the invisible Our Father/Christ/Holy Spirit with his or her spirit eyes.

There are thirty-nine books in the Old Testament and twenty-six books in the New Testament that make up the Bible. Holy Spirit-led Christians living centuries before you to know which books to include in the Bible. These are termed the canon of Scripture and refer to the books written under his inspiration. The thirty-nine books of the Old Testament are the same books that Our Father's Chosen People have in their Scriptures.

There are other writings between the Old and New Testaments, known as the apocryphal books. These books contain some historical facts and truths, but they lack the same inspiration as the books of the Bible. The word apocrypha means hidden because those who read the books cannot determine their purpose. The sixty-six books of the Bible are the only books that will ever be the inspired books of the canon.

* * *

Chapter 9: Living In Two Worlds (Part 3)

THE QUALITY OF LOVE

Let's start the last part of this teaching on living in two worlds, about the quality of love our Father gave you.

2 Corinthians 3:2-3
(King James Version)
2 Ye are our epistle written in our hearts, known and read of all men:
3 Forasmuch as ye are manifestly declared to be the epistle of Christ ministered by us, written not with ink, but with the Spirit of the living God; not in tables of stone, but in fleshy tables of the heart.

The pattern involved in these verses is important to understand. Christ was the author of the letter, Apostle Paul was the scribe, and the

Christians at Corinth were the intended recipients of the letter for others to read. Christ wrote the qualities of His being into their spirits just like Our Father used His finger to engrave the Ten Commandments in two tablets of stone for Our Father's Chosen People. (See Exodus 31:18, 32:16.) 'Your life is the only Bible that some people will ever read." Our Father's plan is that Holy Spirit place some of the qualities of the person of Our Father/Christ/Holy Spirit into the lives of Born-Again Christians. These qualities remain invisible to others until you live your lives by them. When you do this, these invisible qualities become physical realities in your lives that others can see with their own eyes. When you endeavor to put them into practice, regardless of how hard your flesh fights against it, internal suffering is the result as you become the word tried and tested. When Born Again Christians do this, they help others see the invisible Godhead. This not only allows you to become love made perfect, but also allows your love for the king to grow more and more.

1 Peter 5:5
(King James Version)
5 Likewise, ye younger, submit yourselves unto the elder. Yea, all of you be subject one to another, and be clothed with humility: for God resisteth the proud, and giveth grace to the humble.

Of course, you know that Clothes of Humility is something much different than a pastor wearing a robe in the pulpit. Clothes of Humility are the outward actions a Born-Again Christian does because he or she has a Quality of Humility in his or her inner spirit. The Quality of Humility is actually invisible, but the outward expression of one's life based on an inward Quality of Humility is a Quality of Humility that others can see with their physical eyes. "Humility is accepting Our

Father's order of creation. In Humility, we should be concerned about the needs of those around us as we are concerned about our personal needs."

I will use two biblical examples. In these two examples, the outward actions of Humility, based upon an inward Quality of Humility, become Clothes of Humility that others could see with their physical eyes. First of all, the Quality of Humility within our Lord was invisible, but when He tied a towel around Himself and washed the disciples' feet, they saw Humility with their own physical eyes. (See John 13:4.) Secondly, when the innkeeper saw the Good Samaritan take care of one of Our Father's Chosen People who robbers had beaten, the innkeeper saw Humility with his physical eyes. Humility is invisible, but it can be seen when Born Again Christians wear Clothes of Humility."

QUALITIES OF HUMILITY

2 Timothy 3:4
(King James Version)
4 Traitors, heady, highminded, lovers of pleasures more than lovers of God;

A haughty or high-minded person is typically characterized as arrogant rather than humble. On the one hand, Born Again Christians need to have a proper amount of self-respect, but on the other hand, it is important to note that it is even possible for one to place too much emphasis on one's self-importance. Yes, there are even some Born Again Christians who have an exaggerated opinion of the worth of one's abilities.

Romans 4:2-3
(King James Version)
2 For if Abraham were justified by works, he hath whereof to glory; but not before God.
3 For what saith the scripture? Abraham believed God, and it was counted unto him for righteousness.

Patriarch Abraham was saved by faith, not by the works of the law. Since Patriarch Abraham could not save himself by the works of the law, he had nothing to boast about. Since all human beings are sinners, even you who become born-again Christians do not have anything to boast about."

1 John 2:15-17
(King James Version)
15 Love not the world, neither the things that are in the world. If any man love the world, the love of the Father is not in him.
16 For all that is in the world, the lust of the flesh, and the lust of the eyes, and the pride of life, is not of the Father, but is of the world.
17 And the world passeth away, and the lust thereof: but he that doeth the will of God abideth for ever.

The pride of life includes one's clothes, house, furniture, and other Possessions. Since these things are not of eternal quality, they are no reason to be boastful. Because of this, there are times when Born Again Christians do some things that strengthen the demons that are close by: This makes it more difficult for angels to minister to you, and sometimes, as a result, the spiritual warfare is so great that they have to go to the angel field hospital at the church for a while. If you watch violence, greed, and sex on television or read your horoscope, it would be much harder for your Guardian Angels to minister to you. Also, angels cannot live their lives to their fullest potential when they are not living in the environment of Heaven. Even though these two factors affect their life, they are determined to be faithful to the responsibility Our Father has given them, and they will be your Guardian Angel as long as you are living in your physical body.

QUALITIES OF MEEKNESS

Because of the Quality of Meekness in our Father, Holy Spirit had Patriarch Moses write in Deuteronomy 31:6, He will not leave you nor forsake you. This is true for Born Again Christians, both when your circumstances are easy and happy. As well as when your circumstances are troubling and hurtful. Let's use the Lord as an example. "To understand this quality of Our Father in Your Lord, it is important to note that Your Lord could have stopped His life on Planet Earth at any time and returned to Heaven, if He had chosen to do so. This is why, when He was being arrested in the Garden of Gethsemane and Peter tried to defend Him with a sword, your Lord told Peter that He did not need a sword. He told Peter that if he needed help, he could call ten legions of angels. (See Matthew 26:53.) The meekness quality I am communicating about can be seen in Your Lord in that He remained true to His purpose on Planet Earth, even though at times it was hard and painful.

Your Lord was willing to live more than thirty-three years on Earth, where He could not realize His full potential of life because He was not living in the environment of Heaven. It was more important for Your Lord to be doing the work that Our Father sent Him to Planet

Earth to do than it was to realize His full potential in life. (See John 5:36) Therefore, the people could see the Quality of Meekness with their physical eyes because the works of your Lord were based upon this inward Quality of Meekness. "The life of Your Lord on Earth was not always easy, but He never considered returning to Heaven before His mission on Planet Earth was completed. For example, if Your Lord was totally Divine and totally human, He was willing to have all the greatness of His mind and understanding confined in a little microscopic fetus in the womb of His mother. Your Lord was willing to do this so He could fulfill the purpose of Our Father.

Since Your Lord was both totally Divine and totally human while living on Planet Earth, He sometimes suffered pain. When his little body was born out of His mother's womb, as his little lungs filled up with air for the first time, He felt pain and cried, as do all babies. When He played and ran as a child, if He fell, He also ran to His mother for comfort in His hurt. He was a carpenter before he became a preacher, and when he hit his thumb with a hammer, it hurt. (See Mark 6:3.) It was uncomfortable for Your Lord to sleep without a pillow. (See Luke 9:58.) Since Your Lord did not do any miracles for Himself, only for the people, there were times He knew the discomforts of hunger and thirst. Then there were the pains from the beating, the crown of thorns, and the nails in the hands and feet during His trial and crucifixion.

What am I saying? The Quality of Meekness is that your Lord was willing to suffer all these things so that He could do the work Our Father gave Him to do. Listen to me, people of God, the actions that result from your determination to do what Our Father wants you to do, even if this causes you some adversity, affliction, temptation, or persecution, are actions that will let other people see your invisible quality of meekness with their physical eyes."

Hebrews 13:15
(King James Version)
15 By him therefore let us offer the sacrifice of praise to God continually, that is, the fruit of our lips giving thanks to his name.

The praise in this verse is praise to Our Father for salvation. The means of praise are spoken words based on the invisible praise in your inner spirit. The sacrifice of praise is praise to Our Father, even though there are times of adversity, affliction, temptation, and persecution in your life. Such words of praise will permit others around you to see with their physical eyes the invisible Quality of Meekness within you.

THE QUALITY OF MERCY

Being Merciful is another of those invisible qualities of our Father that you can have in your inner spirit, and when you do actions based upon the invisible Quality of Being Merciful, people around you can see this Quality of Being Merciful with their physical eyes. When you received your Measure of Faith when you became a born-again Christian, the ability to be merciful is part of your Measure of Faith. "There are two things that Your Lord is doing for Born Again Christians as He sits at the right hand of Our Father in Heaven. (See Hebrews 4:14-16.) One of the things He is doing is to provide each of you with individual access to Our Father in your times of need. Another thing He is doing is to feel the same infirmities, wants, weaknesses, miseries, and dangers that each of you suffers. Since He suffers with you, as your High Priest in Heaven, He can better intercede for you before Our Father. In these two ways, Your Lord is expressing the Quality of Being Merciful in

Our Father/Christ/Holy Spirit. If you can believe it, this quality of being touched with the feelings of your infirmities also happens to your guardian angels, so that they can minister to you more effectively. "When you became a Born-Again Christian, you received this invisible Quality of Being Merciful from Our Father. Those around you can see the actions you take based on this Quality of Being Merciful. Thus, the Quality of Being Merciful is no longer invisible to them. There are two things to keep in mind as you pattern your life after your High Priest in Heaven, your Lord.

First of all, helping people with their needs as a way of influencing them to let Your Lord also be their High Priest in Heaven should be more important to you than doing the ministry Our Father has given you to do. Secondly, this means you will have to spend time with people who are suffering while praying and interceding for them, so you can begin to feel their suffering to some extent. It is when you are suffering with them that Holy Spirit can lead you in sharing Our Father's Word with them. I can promise you that if you pay closer attention to the Lord, he will lead you to more people who are hurting so that you can begin to taste of people's suffering, thereby becoming a tool for healing. To stay indifferent is to be of no use to the king or the people.

Luke 19:41-44
(King James Version)
41 And when he was come near, he beheld the city, and wept over it,
42 Saying, If thou hadst known, even thou, at least in this thy day, the things which belong unto thy peace! but now they are hid from thine eyes.
43 For the days shall come upon thee, that thine enemies

shall cast a trench about thee, and compass thee round, and keep thee in on every side,
44 And shall lay thee even with the ground, and thy children within thee; and they shall not leave in thee one stone upon another; because thou knewest not the time of thy visitation.

As Your Lord approached Our Father's beloved city, Jerusalem, on the day of His Triumphal Entry, at one point in His journey, He could look out over the city. When He did, He grieved inwardly and outwardly because He knew that there was destruction coming because most of them were rejecting Him as being the Messiah."

John 11:35
(King James Version)
35 Jesus wept.

Your Lord grieved both inwardly and outwardly when his friend, Lazarus, died.

Ephesians 4:30
(King James Version)
30 And grieve not the holy Spirit of God, whereby ye are sealed unto the day of redemption.

Our Father/Christ/Holy Spirit grieves when any one of you Born Again Christians does not obey His Word." So, when you share in the feelings of suffering of others, you are being merciful or compassionate.

This type of sympathy or compassion is necessary for Intercessory Prayer when you read about the instructions that Our Father gave to Patriarch Moses about preparing an ephod for his brother, Aaron, to wear when he went before Our Father to minister to Our Father and to intercede for Our Father's Chosen People. (See Exodus 28:8-12, 29.) The names of the twelve tribes of Our Father's Chosen People were to be engraved on the onyx stones, six names on each stone. This was to be a memorial for Priest Aaron so that he would remember Our Father's Chosen People when he was before Our Father. "Priest Aaron did Intercessory Prayer. Not only did he remember the names on the two onyx stones, but he also felt the sufferings of the people because he was living with them.

Hebrews 7:25
(King James Version)
25 Wherefore he is able also to save them to the uttermost that come unto God by him, seeing he ever liveth to make intercession for them.

```
Your Lord, sitting at the right hand of Our Father in
Heaven, never stops interceding for you. A prayer of
intercession that you pray for someone should not be a
one-time prayer, but a continuing prayer until the answer
comes."
```

Luke 23:34
(King James Version)
34 Then said Jesus, Father, forgive them; for they know not what they do. And they parted his raiment, and cast lots.

Basic prayer for anyone who is not a Born-Again Christian is that the person asks Our Father for forgiveness of sin and becomes saved."

Romans 8:34
(King James Version)
34 Who is he that condemneth? It is Christ that died, yea rather, that is risen again, who is even at the right hand of God, who also maketh intercession for us.

Rather than condemning a sinner or other Born-Again Christians, begin Intercessory Prayer for that person you feel like condemning."

Colossians 1:9-11
(King James Version)
9 For this cause we also, since the day we heard it, do not cease to pray for you, and to desire that ye might be filled with the knowledge of his will in all wisdom and spiritual understanding;
10 That ye might walk worthy of the Lord unto all pleasing, being fruitful in every good work, and increasing in the knowledge of God;
11 Strengthened with all might, according to his glorious power, unto all patience and longsuffering with joyfulness;

In Intercessory Prayer for a Born-Again Christian, you pray for spiritual growth and the meeting of needs. In Intercessory Prayer for those who are not Born Again, you pray that they will be saved so Our Father can meet their needs." These scriptures speak to the mercy that flows from true intercession.

Romans 15:30-32
(King James Version)
30 Now I beseech you, brethren, for the Lord Jesus Christ's sake, and for the love of the Spirit, that ye strive together with me in your prayers to God for me;
31 That I may be delivered from them that do not believe in Judaea; and that my service which I have for Jerusalem may be accepted of the saints;
32 That I may come unto you with joy by the will of God, and may with you be refreshed.

Apostle Paul asked others to have Intercessory Prayer for him. It was time for him to take the money he had raised in offerings for the Church in Jerusalem to Jerusalem. He knew that some of Our Father's Chosen People in Jerusalem were bitterly opposed to him because of the way he presented the Gospel to the Gentiles. So, he asked the Christians in Rome to pray for his safety and that he could fulfill his calling to get to Rome."

OVERCOMING HURT

Because of the quality of faith given to you and love being its most powerful ally, the enemy will constantly try to put you in arms way of the tools that can destroy you, such as the opposite of humility, mercy, and love. Just as those made higher than us, such as the angels they can experience hurt. The source of their hurt is always spiritual warfare with demons. They have learned that they constantly need to be forgiving of the demons for causing them hurt. If that is the case with angels, where does that leave us? We must ensure that we don't become irrelevant to the king. "Most Born Again Christians understand that the Lord died for the sins of all human beings, past, present, and future. It is also true in a very real sense that because His act of dying was an eternal event, through your sins, Born Again Christians help drive the spikes into the hands and feet of Your Lord. (See Hebrews 9:26 and 1 Peter 1:20.) All sinners biblically are considered to be enemies of Our Father. Thus, when Christ died for the sins of all human beings, you were one of those enemies of Your Lord who hurt Him on the Cross. (See Romans 5:8.) Thus, it was when you were born-again Christians that your Lord forgave you of your sins and the hurt you caused Him. Your Lord forgives all human beings, even though He is unjustly hurt, and He knows that not all human beings will accept His Forgiveness. This quality of Your Lord's Forgiveness is one of the invisible qualities of Our Father/Christ/Holy Spirit. Those who are still sinners are still Biblically enemies of Your Lord, and if they are enemies of Your Lord, they are also your enemies. So, when you forgive one of these enemies, the invisible quality of forgiveness becomes visible to the one you forgive.

You should do this forgiving even when you are unjustly hurt, and even when the one hurting you will not receive your Forgiveness. Your act of Forgiveness always makes the invisible quality of the Forgiveness of our Father/Christ/Holy Spirit visible to that person. It should also be noted that you should also be forgiving of any Born-Again Christian who hurts you in a like manner."

1 John 2:2
(King James Version)
2 And he is the propitiation for our sins: and not for ours only, but also for the sins of the whole world.

1 John 5:19
(King James Version)
19 And we know that we are of God, and the whole world lieth in wickedness.

The word world means the world and those who are opposed to Our Father. Your Lord died for Born Again Christians when you were part of the world. You are now part of the Kingdom of Our Father.

Luke 5:24
(King James Version)
24 But that ye may know that the Son of man hath power upon earth to forgive sins, (he said unto the sick of the palsy,) I say unto thee, Arise, and take up thy couch, and go into thine house.

Luke 23:34
(King James Version)
34 Then said Jesus, Father, forgive them; for they know not what they do. And they parted his raiment, and cast lots.

Only Your Lord can actually forgive sins. You can forgive someone for hurting you, but you cannot forgive anyone's sins. Your Lord was more concerned about what the sin was going to do to those who were putting Him to death than He was about the hurt He was receiving.

Mark 11:25-26
(King James Version)
25 And when ye stand praying, forgive, if ye have ought against any: that your Father also which is in heaven may forgive you your trespasses.
26 But if ye do not forgive, neither will your Father which is in heaven forgive your trespasses.

Keep these two things in mind. First of all, when Your Lord was hurt, in this Age of Our Father's Grace, He responded with Forgiveness rather than judgment. Secondly, if you, Born-Again Christians, are to continue to receive Our Father's Forgiveness, you must continue to forgive those who hurt you, both the enemies of Our Father and other Born-Again Christians. The word trespass means to fall short of following the truth.

* * *

V

V. The Gift of Faith

gift
/gift/

a thing given willingly to someone without payment; a present.

Chapter 10: The Gift of Faith

This discussion revolves around the gift of faith; we also want to show the interactions between the seen and unseen worlds as they relate to angels. Angels live in the spirit realm, where there is no quality of time, and we as humans are living on Planet Earth, where there is a quality of time. The angels adapt themselves to our quality of time so that they can minister to us, so let's look at this from our viewpoint of time. There was a time when angels had total freedom of choice while living in Heaven. Then those now known as Satan and fallen angels or demons chose to use their freedom of choice to rebel against Our Father. To stop the rebellion, Our Father started a separation. Our Father did not destroy the rebelling angels, but He separated them from the ones that did not rebel and who continued to obey Our Father. He even created a place called Hell as their home. After this separation was completed, the angels that did not rebel found that they could no longer make a free will choice to disobey Our Father. You need to remember that angels were and are living without the factor of time. Therefore, what you call past, present, and future is like an ongoing present moment for them. (I know that it is hard to comprehend when you consider that time is something that our father created, then superimposed within the fabric of our lives). Although they cannot make a decision now to disobey Our Father, they have the freedom of choice because the meaning of their decision to continue obeying Our Father is always present in their experience of existence. I know that's a mouthful, but that's the way Holy Spirit explained it to me.

DIFFERENCE OF OPINION

There is a difference of theological opinion among Born Again Christians in this matter, but I will not discuss this difference of opinion. Rather, there is one important point I am going to make. When you became a Born-Again Christian, you learned that you needed to begin separating yourself from sin and from those who disobeyed Our Father. This has only been a partial separation for you, as you are still living among sin and those who disobey Our Father. For example, you are to be fellowshipping with those who are Born Again Christians, while you are still having lesser levels of relationships with those who are disobeying Our Father. Your separation from those who are disobeying Our Father and sin will not be complete until your experience of the physical death resurrection event, or the short version, the Rapture. Then your separation from sin and those who disobey Our Father will be complete, and you will no longer be able to make a decision to disobey Our Father. At that time, you will be like the angels and live in the eternal realm, beyond the quality of time. Though you will not be able to make a choice to disobey Our Father, you will continue to have the meaning of making free-will choices because you will have the memories of free-will choices with you, like the angels. For you, your life will be like an ongoing moment of all the past, present, and future of your life. This speaks to some of the likenesses you will experience that Christ spoke of when he said you will be as the angels; that statement had more than one meaning.

2 Corinthians 6:11-18
(King James Version)

11 O ye Corinthians, our mouth is open unto you, our heart is enlarged.
12 Ye are not straitened in us, but ye are straitened in your own bowels.
13 Now for a recompence in the same, (I speak as unto my children,) be ye also enlarged.
14 Be ye not unequally yoked together with unbelievers: for what fellowship hath righteousness with unrighteousness? and what communion hath light with darkness?
15 And what concord hath Christ with Belial? or what part hath he that believeth with an infidel?
16 And what agreement hath the temple of God with idols? for ye are the temple of the living God; as God hath said, I will dwell in them, and walk in them; and I will be their God, and they shall be my people.
17 Wherefore come out from among them, and be ye separate, saith the Lord, and touch not the unclean thing; and I will receive you.
18 And will be a Father unto you, and ye shall be my sons and daughters, saith the Lord Almighty.

We have discussed how all humans are endowed with faith to help us navigate this natural world, which we refer to as intuition, and how our Father bestows talents upon humans to advance the human race. We also spoke about a Measure of Faith when you became a Born-Again

Christian, but you also received a Gift of Faith. The Gift of Faith is about power. The Gift of Faith gives you the power to keep yourself separated from sin and those who keep disobeying Our Father. Your Lord told those observing the ascension to return to Jerusalem and pray until they received Holy Spirit in a new way, and he gave them power to be witnesses. Remember on the Day of Pentecost, the people in Jerusalem observed the lives of those coming out of the upper room before Apostle Peter stood up and spoke words of witnessing. This is an example that the first power you receive from the Gift of Faith is the power to live your Christian life." I know we are looking at the gift of faith in a way that you may not have heard it taught before, because many only hear about it in retrospect to the nine gifts. Well, the scripture says they are given to every man as he wills, not just preachers. However, this is the first way the gift of faith manifests in the life of a Spirit-filled believer.

Galatians 2:20
(King James Version)
20 I am crucified with Christ: nevertheless I live; yet not I, but Christ liveth in me: and the life which I now live in the flesh I live by the faith of the Son of God, who loved me, and gave himself for me.

2 Corinthians 13:4
(King James Version)
4 For though he was crucified through weakness, yet he liveth by the power of God. For we also are weak in him, but we shall live with him by the power of God toward you.

I want you to notice, in verse 20, the faith of the Son of God, and, in verse 4, living by the raw power of God. The faith in God comes through the measure of faith as one grows, believes, and feeds on the word of God. The faith of God is the gift of faith, the raw power of God given to you when you believe that you can resist sin when you make the effort. This is where the fine line is and why many people do not want to stop sinning. Your flesh likes a particular thing, and you enjoy it, and while that happens, you will not resist. You must die to that thing you enjoy. "Through the Gift of Faith Holy Spirit gives Born Again Christians the power to keep their lives free from sin. For example, the power in the Gift of Faith is great enough to discipline any physical desire your human body may ever have." (only if your will is resisting)

Romans 6:6
(King James Version)
6 Knowing this, that our old man is crucified with him, that the body of sin might be destroyed, that henceforth we should not serve sin.

```
Notice what he said, the body of sin might be destroyed, you
have been given the ability to destroy it, but you cannot
destroy it and want it at the same time.
```

Romans 6:12-14
(King James Version)
12 Let not sin therefore reign in your mortal body, that ye should obey it in the lusts thereof. (lust means pressure, when the enemy puts pressure on your weakness)
13 Neither yield ye your members as instruments of unrighteousness unto sin: but yield yourselves unto God, as

those that are alive from the dead, and your members as instruments of righteousness unto God. (you can yield them when you resist)
14 For sin shall not have dominion over you: for ye are not under the law, but under grace.

Holy Spirit had the Apostle Paul write about you having dominion over sin; he used a verb that means to continue exercising that dominion. Simply put, when you resist power flows.

POWER TO WITNESS

The first thing you received power for is to be a witness. We also mentioned that the beginning of the witness is to use the power of the Gift of Faith to keep your life free from sin and to live a Christian life. Thus, the life you are living is one way of witnessing. The meaning of the Greek word translated as 'witness' is one who is a spectator and gives an account of what they saw.

Acts 2:32
(King James Version)
32 This Jesus hath God raised up, whereof we all are witnesses.

Apostle Peter shared his experiences of seeing Your Lord in His resurrected body after His Resurrection. Keep in mind that, even though you are seeing your Lord with your spirit, yes, in worship and prayer, or in an occasional vision, you are seeing Him after His Resurrection.

Acts 5:31-32

(King James Version)

31 Him hath God exalted with his right hand to be a Prince and a Saviour, for to give repentance to Israel, and forgiveness of sins.

32 And we are his witnesses of these things; and so is also the Holy Ghost, whom God hath given to them that obey him.

The mission of Your Lord while on Planet Earth was to give repentance and forgiveness of sin, first to Our Father's Chosen People, and then to the Gentiles. If and when you see the Lord in visions or dreams, it becomes a part of your mission to share with others about seeing him; this is part of your witness.

Acts 1:21-22

(King James Version)

21 Wherefore of these men which have companied with us all the time that the Lord Jesus went in and out among us,

22 Beginning from the baptism of John, unto that same day that he was taken up from us, must one be ordained to be a witness with us of his resurrection.

When the eleven Apostles selected a successor to Judas Iscariot, they were instructed to select someone who had seen Your Lord's Baptism, Ministry, Resurrection, and Ascension into heaven. Such a person could testify that Your Lord was alive even though He was crucified. Because you see Your Lord with your spirit eyes in worship and prayer, you can give witness that He is alive and well.

1 Peter 5:1
(King James Version)
5 The elders which are among you I exhort, who am also an elder, and a witness of the sufferings of Christ, and also a partaker of the glory that shall be revealed:

When you realize that your sins help drive the spikes into the hands and feet of Your Lord, as you see Him with your spirit eyes in your worship and prayer, you also see His suffering for you and all people. Thus, a part of your verbal witness is about the sufferings of Your Lord.

* * *

Chapter 11: The Gift of Faith (Part 2)

There are no such things as non-essential Biblical truths. All truths that are in the Bible are essential, and one truth is as important as the other. As you held on to the truths of your Born-Again Experience, the miracle conception of Jesus, and the bodily Resurrection of your Lord, you were using some of the power you received from Holy Spirit in the Gift of Faith you received when you became a Born-Again Christian. This power gave you the courage and ability to hold on to your beliefs in these matters even though others may have tried to encourage you to believe otherwise. This is the meaning of a word that is translated to stand in the New Testament. This means that when you find a Biblical truth, you hold on to it, you continue to believe and base your life upon it."

1 Corinthians 2:4-8
(King James Version)
4 And my speech and my preaching was not with enticing words of man's wisdom, but in demonstration of the Spirit

and of power:
5 That your faith should not stand in the wisdom of men, but in the power of God.
6 Howbeit we speak wisdom among them that are perfect: yet not the wisdom of this world, nor of the princes of this world, that come to nought:
7 But we speak the wisdom of God in a mystery, even the hidden wisdom, which God ordained before the world unto our glory:
8 Which none of the princes of this world knew: for had they known it, they would not have crucified the Lord of glory.

1 Corinthians 15:1
(King James Version)
15 Moreover, brethren, I declare unto you the gospel which I preached unto you, which also ye have received, and wherein ye stand;

The Gift of Faith includes power to understand and to preach and teach the wisdom of Our Father. Once you learn the wisdom of Our Father, take a stand for it."

John 8:32
(King James Version)
32 And ye shall know the truth, and the truth shall make you free.

Galatians 5:1

(King James Version)
5 Stand fast therefore in the liberty wherewith Christ hath made us free, and be not entangled again with the yoke of bondage.

Once you are set free by the truth of Our Father, take a stand for the truth of Our Father."

Colossians 4:12
(King James Version)
12 Epaphras, who is one of you, a servant of Christ, saluteth you, always labouring fervently for you in prayers, that ye may stand perfect and complete in all the will of God.

When you find the will of Our Father for your life, take a stand "for the will of Our Father in your life.

Romans 11:20
(King James Version)
20 Well; because of unbelief they were broken off, and thou standest by faith. Be not high-minded, but fear:

When you, Born Again Christians, take on the humility of Your Lord, take a stand and do not become proud and haughty."

WALKING BY FAITH

2 Corinthians 5:7
(King James Version)
7 (For we walk by faith, not by sight:)

Our Father has given some the privilege of occasionally seeing into the spirit realm by opening their spirit eyes. Then there are fewer who see into that realm all the time; however, you may not have that gift, so that requires you to walk by faith, and that is what happens when you become born again. Since you could not use your physical eyes to see where you were walking in the spirit realm, when you were Born Again, you received a Gift of Faith so that you could walk in the spirit realm around you. Our Father's basic plan is that Born Again Christians use their physical eyes to walk in the natural world around them and use their Gift of Faith to walk in the spirit realm around them. "Since Your Lord is seated at the right hand of Our Father in Heaven, Holy Spirit, walk with you as you live your life, both in the natural realm and the spirit realm.

In Deuteronomy 31:6, the Bible says that he will never leave you or forsake you unless you walk into places without the express permission of Holy Spirit, such as porno stores, liquor stores, and abortion clinics.

Romans 6:4-9
(King James Version)
4 Therefore we are buried with him by baptism into death:
that like as Christ was raised up from the dead by the glory
of the Father, even so we also should walk in newness of life.
5 For if we have been planted together in the likeness of his
death, we shall be also in the likeness of his resurrection:

6 Knowing this, that our old man is crucified with him, that the body of sin might be destroyed, that henceforth we should not serve sin.
7 For he that is dead is freed from sin.
8 Now if we be dead with Christ, we believe that we shall also live with him:
9 Knowing that Christ being raised from the dead dieth no more; death hath no more dominion over him.

When you became a Born-Again Christian, you began to enjoy the blessings of Heaven even though you were and are still living in the confinement of your physical body and Planet Earth. The power that comes to you through the Gift of Faith enables you to continue to enjoy the blessings of Heaven until you get to Heaven, free from the confinement of your physical body and Planet Earth. The newness of life is about knowing that, with every new day, you gain new experiences. The meaning of Your Gift of Faith needs to be added to each one of these new experiences. (That means bring heaven to earth through your gift of faith.)

Psalm 1:1-2
(King James Version)
1 Blessed is the man that walketh not in the counsel of the ungodly, nor standeth in the way of sinners, nor sitteth in the seat of the scornful.
2 But his delight is in the law of the Lord; and in his law doth he meditate day and night.

```
Every single day, you need to add the meaning of the Ten
Commandments to each new experience that comes into your
life." Let's say it a different way, you need to take the
opportunity to obey the word of God every time an
opportunity comes, to do otherwise.
```

Ephesians 5:16
(King James Version)
16 Redeeming the time, because the days are evil.
Colossians 4:5
(King James Version)
5 Walk in wisdom toward them that are without,
redeeming the time.

MAINTAINING A GOOD REPORT THROUGH FAITH

The reason that time needs to be redeemed is that Satan knows how to use time and will use your time if you do not keep him from doing so. The power that you receive from your Gift of Faith enables you to keep Satan from doing with your time what he wants to do. It is important for you to understand that walking in faith also means making a point of doing with your time what Our Father wants you to do, and not doing with your time what Satan wants you to do.

Because Born Again Christians continue to live on Earth where there is both good and evil, there are times when you do have some difficult, troubling, and painful times. It is important that you learn how to always give a good report as a witness to those who are not Yet Born again. Your Gift of Faith will enable you to always give good reports.

1 Timothy 3:7
(King James Version)
7 Moreover he must have a good report of them which are without; lest he fall into reproach and the snare of the devil.

One Biblical example of this is when Patriarch Moses sent twelve men on a reconnaissance mission into the Promised Land. (See Numbers 13:1-33.) All twelve men returned with raving reports about the abundance of food in the land, but there were both good and bad reports. Ten men examined the responsibility of human beings to possess the land and issued a negative report. They even exaggerated the size of the men living in the land and the fortifications of the land, and said that Our Father's Chosen People would not be able to possess the land. Two of the men, Caleb and Joshua, had their minds on Our Father's promise, and gave a good report that the land could be possessed. (See Numbers 13:30; 14:6-9.) Because our Father is greater than Satan, good is greater than evil, Born-Again Christians can always give a good report about every event and circumstance in their lives. You will not even have to exaggerate to do this." It does not matter how things appear; if you are living by our fathers' word, you can claim his promises by the quality of faith that resides inside you, and it will bring the power of God on the scene.

Hebrews 11:1-3;39
(King James Version)
11 Now faith is the substance of things hoped for, the evidence of things not seen.
2 For by it the elders obtained a good report.
3 Through faith we understand that the worlds were framed by the word of God, so that things which are seen were not made of things which do appear.

39 And these all, having obtained a good report through faith, received not the promise:

Even though some Old Testament saints went through very difficult times, they gave a good report. The reason they gave a good report is because they knew that Our Father was the creator of them and Planet Earth, and since He was the creator, He would sustain their lives according to His purposes for them."

Isaiah 53:1

(King James Version)

53 Who hath believed our report? and to whom is the arm of the Lord revealed?

People of Old Testament times could also give a good report because Holy Spirit was letting them know that the Deliverer Messiah was coming to them.

Acts 1:11

(King James Version)

11 Which also said, Ye men of Galilee, why stand ye gazing up into heaven? this same Jesus, which is taken up from you into heaven, shall so come in like manner as ye have seen him go into heaven.

Born Again Christians can always give a good report because you know that your Deliverer, Messiah, will again come from Heaven.

John 14:1-3
(King James Version)
14 Let not your heart be troubled: ye believe in God, believe also in me.
2 In my Father's house are many mansions: if it were not so, I would have told you. I go to prepare a place for you.
3 And if I go and prepare a place for you, I will come again, and receive you unto myself; that where I am, there ye may be also.

Born Again Christians can always give a good report because they know that if the events of life result in their physical death, they will go to Heaven. And Holy Spirit will take care of you until you get there.

OVERCOMING THE WORLD

We can also see from the word that our father's intentions for us are to overcome the world; this is another reason we possess the quality of faith that we do. Remember, the word world" means the universe and those opposed to Our Father. If you, as a Born-Again Christian, are more concerned about being the person whom Our Father has created you to be than a type of person you may want to be, Holy Spirit can use the Gift of Faith within you to strengthen you in such a way that you can overcome the world. If you have a greater desire to obtain meaning from the spirit realm than you do in obtaining material possessions, Holy Spirit can use your Gift of Faith in such a way as to empower you to overcome the world. "Actually, the definition of overcoming the world is very simple. Overcoming those things within you and around you that could hinder you in doing the Ten Commandments is overcoming the world. You can do this as Holy Spirit empowers you through your Gift of Faith to do this."

1 John 4:4
(King James Version)
4 Ye are of God, little children, and have overcome them: because greater is he that is in you, than he that is in the world.

Now you see it is through the gift of faith that the greater one impowers you.

1 John 5:4-5
(King James Version)
4 For whatsoever is born of God overcometh the world: and this is the victory that overcometh the world, even our faith.
5 Who is he that overcometh the world, but he that believeth that Jesus is the Son of God?

The Greek verb form for overcoming is a continuous action verb. Thus, this is not only about overcoming each event in life, but it is also about overcoming until you go to Heaven. Satan is the one who tries to hinder you so that you will not be able to overcome. Not only is overcoming about Holy Spirit working in you, but it is also about your commitment to the purpose of overcoming. The following verses are about some of the results of overcoming: Revelation 2:7, 2:11, 2:26, 3:5, 3:12, and 3:21.

OVERCOMING SATAN

The 91st Psalm is a lesson on how to let the angels help us overcome Satan in so many ways. "According to the first verse of this Psalm, this blessing is for one who is living under the Shadow of the Almighty. In this Church Age, this means a Born-Again Christian living their life according to the ways of Our Father. This means that such a person is keeping their life in a place where the angels can minister to them. The expression "in all your ways" refers to experiences that are dangerous and those that are not. In other words, angels will minister to a person in all of his or her experiences of life."

1 Timothy 6:6-12
(King James Version)
6 But godliness with contentment is great gain. 7 For we
brought nothing into this world, and it is certain we can
carry nothing out. 8 And having food and raiment let us be
therewith content. 9 But they that will be rich fall into
temptation and a snare, and into many foolish and hurtful
lusts, which drown men in destruction and perdition. 10 For
the love of money is the root of all evil: which while some
coveted after, they have erred from the faith, and pierced
themselves through with many sorrows. 11 But thou, O man
of God, flee these things; and follow after righteousness,
godliness, faith, love, patience, meekness. 12 Fight the good
fight of faith, lay hold on eternal life, whereunto thou art
also called, and hast professed a good profession before

many witnesses.

The fight involves disciplining your physical desires so that you do not seek money to satisfy your body's desires more than you seek the spiritual qualities of life and Heaven. If you commit yourself to doing this, then through the Gift of Faith you received when you became a born-again Christian, Holy Spirit will be able to give you the ability and strength to discipline the human part of you. This is also important, for if you discipline your human side, your angels will be able to overcome the demons that come to you. Our Father's plan is that your angels fight these demons for you. If this is happening in your life, then you can know that even those things that appear to be negative that happen to you are all in the purpose of Our Father. You are to fight the battle of discipline; angels are to fight the demons.

Ephesians 6:6-20
(King James Version)

***6 Not with eyeservice, as menpleasers; but as the servants of
Christ, doing the will of God from the heart; 7 With good
will doing service, as to the Lord, and not to men: 8
Knowing that whatsoever good thing any man doeth, the
same shall he receive of the Lord, whether he be bond or
free. 9 And, ye masters, do the same things unto them,
forbearing threatening: knowing that your Master also is
in heaven; neither is there respect of persons with him. 10
Finally, my brethren, be strong in the Lord, and in the
power of his might. 11 Put on the whole armour of God, that
ye may be able to stand against the wiles of the devil. 12 For
we wrestle not against flesh and blood, but against
principalities, against powers, against the rulers of the
darkness of this world, against spiritual wickedness in high***

***places. 13 Wherefore take unto you the whole armour of
God, that ye may be able to withstand in the evil day, and
having done all, to stand. 14 Stand therefore, having your
loins girt about with truth, and having on the breastplate
of righteousness; 15 And your feet shod with the
preparation of the gospel of peace; 16 Above all, taking the
shield of faith, wherewith ye shall be able to quench all the
fiery darts of the wicked. 17 And take the helmet of
salvation, and the sword of the Spirit, which is the word of
God: 18 Praying always with all prayer and supplication in
the Spirit, and watching thereunto with all perseverance
and supplication for all saints; 19 And for me, that
utterance may be given unto me, that I may open my mouth
boldly, to make known the mystery of the gospel, 20 For
which I am an ambassador in bonds: that therein I may
speak boldly, as I ought to speak.***

In these verses, the Whole Armor of God is presented as a spiritual quality that you put on your spiritual being every day. You are actually putting on the Whole Armor of God when you discipline the human part of you according to the instructions Our Father has given you in His Word. When you do this, your angels will be able to do spiritual warfare on your behalf, and through your Gift of Faith, you will be able to do your part in overcoming Satan and demons. Remember, you are to fight the battle of discipline and the angels, the demons.

Revelation 12:11
(King James Version)
11 And they overcame him by the blood of the Lamb, and by the word of their testimony; and they loved not their lives unto the death.

This guideline verse for overcoming Satan is more about how you discipline your life than it is about pleading the Blood of Jesus. There are three areas of discipline Holy Spirit mentioned in this verse. 1) Blood of the Lamb is about having sin cleansed from your life as you are a born-again Christian. 2) The word of their testimony is about living one's life according to the Word of Our Father and also worshipping Our Father. 3) They did not love their lives to the death means that you are to be more concerned about getting to Heaven than you are about being a survivor on Planet Earth.

Again, when you fight the fight of disciplining your life in these ways, your angels will fight the fight of doing spiritual warfare for you.

* * *

VI

VI. Dunamis Power

pow·er
*/ˈ**pou**(ə)**r**/*

the ability to do something or act in a particular way,
especially as a faculty or quality.

Chapter 12: Dunamis Power

As you know, I like giving examples, or what the bible calls parables, to make the word easier to see, not more difficult. With that said, let's look at the example of oranges gathering some of the sun's energy, and when you eat the oranges, you receive that energy into your body. Among the energy items in the orange is vitamin C, which helps your body overcome some of the effects of chemicals your body receives from secondhand cigarette smoke and environmental pollutants. These are things that sometimes cause cancer. In this parable, the sun is Our Father. Eating an orange represents taking Holy Spirit into your being. The energy in the orange represents the power of Our Father that Holy Spirit refers to in the New Testament as ***Dunamis.*** We all have Spirit Light Energy that we received from Our Father. This Spirit Light Energy coming from Our Father is called ***Dunamis*** and contains healing qualities.

On the Mount of Transfiguration, Peter, James, and John saw Your Lord temporarily in His light form so that they would be able to recognize Him after His Resurrection. (See Matthew 17:2.) The angel that rolled the stone away from the entrance of the tomb where Your Lord was lying appeared in his spirit light form. (See Matthew 28:2-3.) Right before Deacon Stephen began to reply to the charge of blasphemy placed against him, those who were there that day saw his face begin to look like an angel's, that is, he began to become a spirit-light form being. (See Acts. 6:15.)" You recall, in the Gospel of Luke, Holy Spirit had Apostle Luke record about a woman who had a hemorrhaging problem for twelve years, and the doctors were not able to bring about her cure. One day, in a crowd, this lady reached out and touched the hem of the garment our Lord was wearing, and she was healed. What did the Lord say after her miracle healing took place?

Luke 8:46

(King James Version)

46 And Jesus said, Somebody hath touched me: for I perceive that virtue is gone out of me.

The Greek word translated as power or virtue is ***Dunamis***. That day, the Spirit Light Energy of Our Father flowed from Your Lord to the lady, and her miracle resulted. That is exactly what it looked like if you saw it in the spirit realm, light. The Gift of Faith you received when you became a Bom Again Christian has the capability of receiving the Spirit Light Power (Dunamis) of Our Father into your life."

Luke 4:36

(King James Version)

36 And they were all amazed, and spake among themselves, saying, What a word is this! for with authority and power he commandeth the unclean spirits, and they come out.

```
The spirit energy of the Dunamis Power brought about every
miracle that Your Lord did.
```

Luke 24:49
(King James Version)
49 And, behold, I send the promise of my Father upon you: but tarry ye in the city of Jerusalem, until ye be endued with power from on high.

```
Everyone who becomes a Born-Again Christian receives the
following Measure of Faith, and the Gift of Faith, when one
is filled with Holy Spirit. He has the Spirit Energy of
Dunamis Power within him. This Spirit Energy is what
miraculously removed a deadly virus from my body after I
came back from Nigeria.
```

THE LIGHT POWER OF ANGELS

When it comes to this light, we are making references to. Let's look at angels in comparison. 'As you know, angels are spirit light beings, and you are a spirit light being living in a human body. In the Bible, Holy Spirit had a unique description of Cherub Angels. (See Ezekiel 1:13-14.) The spirit light form of the Cherub Angels is described as burning coals of fire. These angels also have Spirit Light Energy, and so do you. The encouragement for you to learn in this lesson is that the angels who are ministering to you have much greater Spirit Light Energy than you do. So, in this respect, the ministering angels are greater than you. When you get to Heaven, no longer confined in a human body, your Spirit Light Energy will be similar to that of the angels. (See Matthew 22:30.) "Now let's think about the comparison of a kerosene lamp we used to use for light back in the day, which was equivalent to about 10 watts of energy, and a one-hundred-watt electric light bulb in your house today. In that comparison, you have the light energy of a kerosene lamp representing your Spirit Light Energy, and the light of a one-hundred-watt light bulb representing the Spirit Light Energy of one of your Guardian Angels. Thus, Our Father is using Guardian Angels to extend his Dunamis Power to you because the angels have much greater Spirit Light Energy than born-again Christians.

Matthew 27:60
(King James Version)
60 And laid it in his own new tomb, which he had hewn out in the rock: and he rolled a great stone to the door of the sepulchre, and departed.

Matthew 28:2
(King James Version)
2 And, behold, there was a great earthquake: for the angel of the Lord descended from heaven, and came and rolled back the stone from the door, and sat upon it.

As Joseph of Arimathea oversaw the burial of Your Lord, it took several men to roll the huge stone into place to close the entrance to the tomb where Your Lord was laid after His crucifixion. Still, it only took one angel to roll the stone away so the women could look into the tomb and see that Your Lord had been resurrected.

Psalm 103:20-22
(King James Version)
20 Bless the Lord, ye his angels, that excel in strength, that do his commandments, hearkening unto the voice of his word.
21 Bless ye the Lord, all ye his hosts; ye ministers of his, that do his pleasure.
22 Bless the Lord, all his works in all places of his dominion: bless the Lord, O my soul.

In this passage, it is not only stated that angels are great, implying they are greater than you, human beings, but also that angels can give greater worship to Our Father than you, Born Again Christians, still living in your human bodies. Today, some Christian preachers and teachers suggest that angels cannot praise Our Father for redemption because the angels have not sinned. These seem to be saying that because you, Born Again Christians, experience Our Father's redemption, you can worship Our Father better than the angels in this one way. This is kind of like saying that a person who has been saved from and delivered from some major sins better understands Our Father's love than one who grows up in a Christian home and does not commit any major sins. The problem with that reasoning is that those who are saved and delivered from great sins still have memories of those sins, which greatly hinder their worship. These memories of sin will not be erased until they reach Heaven. (This is the contrast between us and angels.)

Revelation 5:8-10
(King James Version)
8 And when he had taken the book, the four beasts and four and twenty elders fell down before the Lamb, having every one of them harps, and golden vials full of odours, which

are the prayers of saints.
9 And they sung a new song, saying, Thou art worthy to take the book, and to open the seals thereof: for thou wast slain, and hast redeemed us to God by thy blood out of every kindred, and tongue, and people, and nation;
10 And hast made us unto our God kings and priests: and we shall reign on the earth.

Note that both angels and saints are worshipping Our Father in Heaven for His redemptive character. In experiencing compassion for humans in their sins, angels know more about Our Father's love than humans will ever know while still living in their human bodies. Angels do not think about I and me. They only think of 'we' and 'us'. As they think of 'we' and 'us', they think of all created spirit beings, both angels and human beings. The angels who are ministering Our Father's Dunamis Power for Born Again Christians are far greater beings than human beings.

ANOTHER DIFFERENCE

When Our Father created angels, he made them light beings that are imperishable. When He created human beings, He made them imperishable light beings living in perishable human bodies. When you were born in your mother's womb, you were born of corruptible or perishable seed. When you became a Born-Again Christian, you were born of incorruptible imperishable seed. (See 1 Peter 1:23.) Angels experienced being created, but they did not experience being born of corruptible seeds and living in perishable bodies.

Our Father created Adam and Eve, and he also created a seed-planting process so that the perishable human bodies of humans can continue through offspring forming in a mother's womb. In fact, the seed-planting process was for all forms of life on Planet Earth, including both animal and plant life forms. When a seed is properly planted, the seed will produce an offspring that is very much like the one who planted the seed. When a seed is properly planted, the Dunamis Power of Our Father creates or produces an offspring. For example, when Adam planted a seed in his wife, Eve, she knew that the offspring she carried in her womb was from Our Father. (See Genesis 4:1.) Children that are created from seeds in mothers' wombs are fruits of the womb. (See Psalm 127:3.)

My Grandfather planted some wheat seed every year on his farm. Before hybrid seeds were developed, he would select some of his best wheat grains from the previous harvest and use them as wheat seeds. He and other farmers used a seed sifter to prepare the wheat seeds. The seed sifter was a machine in a wooden box about five feet square. Inside was a bottom screen with another screen two feet above it. Each screen had different-sized holes. When wheat grains were fed into the machine, the two screens would move back and forth, air would be forced through the machine, and any weed seeds harvested with the wheat would be separated from the wheat grains. This gave him clean wheat seeds to plant. If he did not plant clean wheat seeds each season, he would have been harvesting as many weed seeds as wheat. "When the Dunamis Power of Our Father produces a fruit of the womb from a seed planted in a mother's womb, it is certainly a great blessing. Now note this. There are clean seeds and unclean seeds that can be planted in a mother's womb. The clean seed comes from one man and one woman in a married relationship. When a seed is planted by any other means, such as pre-marital seed planting and extra-marital affair seed planting, the seed is unclean. What does that mean? One can make a child more susceptible to darkness in the form of curses and diseases. Being born with a flawed seed can make the child more accountable when they should be living in a time of grace or unaccountability when it comes to sin. Since their life has just begun, it is not the child's sins, but those of the parent.

Based upon the understanding of the Old Testament saints, Our Father's Chosen People knew that because original sin is passed to each fruit of the womb through the seed, the mother is unclean after the fruit of the womb is born. This did not mean that the mother was sinful, but rather that she could not approach Our Father in worship until she underwent a rite of purification. (See Leviticus 12:2, 4.) Also note that no more seed was to be planted until after the rite of purification. "Since forgiveness of sin is provided for by Your Lord dying on the Cross as the Blood Sacrifice for sin, the approach of the New Testament is different in this matter. Under the new covenant, the blood of Jesus has already forgiven and cleansed the mother regardless of what comes out of her womb.

Hebrews 13:4
(King James Version)
4 Marriage is honourable in all, and the bed undefiled: but whoremongers and adulterers God will judge.

Let's say it a different way. The word conceived means planting a seed. When both couples were married during childbearing, their experiences were similar to those of Our Father's Chosen People in Old Testament times, but they were also very different. The similarity was that each fruit of the womb received original sin through the seed, which was spiritual death. The difference is because both husband and wife are born again and are blessed by the Dunamis Power of

Our Father working through Gifts of Faith; the wife did not become unclean when she conceived.

```
This means that one of the great blessings of the Dunamis
Power of Our Father functioning in the lives of Born Again
Christians is that for one man and one woman, their marriage
bed is holy when clean seed is being planted.
```

* * *

Chapter 13: Dumanis Power (Part 2)

One of the purposes of the Dunamis Power of Our Father that comes to you through Holy Spirit and the Gift of Faith in you is to heal your spirit of the disease of sin in your inner spirit. Another purpose of this Dunamis Power is to cleanse your outward life from any sinful activities that you are doing. Even when you were a young child, most likely in Sunday school, you were taught that you not only needed to be forgiven of your sins, but also to have your life cleansed of any sinful activity you were engaging in. Both realities need to happen for one to be made totally whole by your Lord.

Luke 8:48
(King James Version)
48 And he said unto her, Daughter, be of good comfort: thy faith hath made thee whole; go in peace.

```
After the lady who had the issue of blood touched the hem of
the garment of Your Lord, and Dunamis Power went out of Him,
He told her that her faith had made her well. The Greek word
translated whole or well means to become well in one's
spirit, soul, body, and circumstances of life.
```

Ephesians 2:8
(King James Version)
8 For by grace are ye saved through faith; and that not of yourselves: it is the gift of God:

The word translated "saved" in this verse is the same as the word translated "whole" in Luke 8:48. This is about being healed of sin in one's inner spirit. Now, there is a caution to note here. Many Born Again Christians, after reflecting on the meaning of being forgiven of sin, begin to think about the healing of their bodies and the circumstances of their lives, but there is something else that should also take place. Note this in the next Scripture.

Matthew 8:1-4
(King James Version)
8 When he was come down from the mountain, great multitudes followed him.
2 And, behold, there came a leper and worshipped him, saying, Lord, if thou wilt, thou canst make me clean.
3 And Jesus put forth his hand, and touched him, saying, I will; be thou clean. And immediately his leprosy was cleansed.
4 And Jesus saith unto him, See thou tell no man; but go thy way, shew thyself to the priest, and offer the gift that Moses

commanded, for a testimony unto them.

Since the man with leprosy was healed when Your Lord touched him, the man was healed when Dunamis Power went to him from Your Lord. Although a miracle of healing resulted, the word used to describe what happened is different from the one used to describe the lady who was healed of the issue of blood. The word describing the healing of the leper meant to cleanse, not to make whole or well. The meaning of unclean in the Bible is something that separates one from Our Father, so that one cannot worship Our Father. In Bible times, lepers were isolated from other people, termed unclean, and had to live in groups all by themselves so they could not touch or fellowship with other people. If the man healed from leprosy was pronounced to be clean by the priest, then he could again fellowship with and touch other human beings. In a spiritual sense, outward sins render a person unclean, preventing them from fellowshipping with or worshiping Our Father. Thus, one of Dunamis Power's important purposes is to cleanse people of outward sins. However, keep in mind that if one allows sin to remain in their life for any length of time, it can harm one's spirit, which will eventually lead to physical illness.

WHERE ARE YOU SICK?

When your children, grandchildren, or family members are sick, you need to determine where they are sick. I want to reiterate that you're not just a physical being; you're a spiritual being, and the symptoms or signs were different. When their human bodies are ill, the symptoms typically include runny noses, coughs, sore throats, fevers, rashes, earaches, and other similar ailments. When they had bad dreams, were unusually afraid of the dark, seemed more anxious than usual, and were quieter and withdrawn than usual, you know that something is troubling them in the spiritual part of them. When their bodies were ill, we often sought the help of a doctor. When their spirit beings within them had a problem, we used a lot of conversation and prayer. Even though you are a Born-Again Christian, sickness can take place both in your spiritual being and your human body. You need to discern the difference because Our Father uses spiritual laws to heal the spiritual aspect and typically employs natural laws to heal the physical aspect. I want to emphasize the healing of the spirit being part through the Dunamis Power that Holy Spirit places in you through your Gift of Faith. "The healing of your spirit man began when you received forgiveness of your sin by your Lord when you became a born-again Christian. This healing continues to be extended to your emotions and mind. These healings of the spirit being in your human body involve the spiritual laws Our Father has created for spirit beings, not the natural laws created for healing physical bodies of you, human beings. "There are a few times when healing involves both the human body and spirit being of a person. Such as one becoming an alcoholic, the main reason was an emotional problem in the spirit being of a person. A person who is an alcoholic usually has a feeling of inferiority that results in a feeling of extreme depression. This person then begins to quit the feeling of depression by deadening his or her feelings with alcohol. Alcohol can eventually have a negative effect on the brain and liver of the person.

If such a person becomes a Born-Again Christian and their spirit is healed from the sickness of sin, then Holy Spirit can begin to use Dunamis Power to heal the inferiority problem in their spirit and the physical problems in their body. Holy Spirit will use spiritual laws to heal the spirit being part and usually will use natural laws to heal the physical body part. Yes, he can use Dunamis power to activate the natural laws he put within the body to heal itself, which is called a miracle.

2 Corinthians 12:9-10
(King James Version)
9 And he said unto me, My grace is sufficient for thee: for my strength is made perfect in weakness. Most gladly therefore will I rather glory in my infirmities, that the power of Christ may rest upon me.
10 Therefore I take pleasure in infirmities, in reproaches, in necessities, in persecutions, in distresses for Christ's sake: for when I am weak, then am I strong.

Infirmities, reproaches, needs, persecutions, and distresses are problems that Satan put upon Apostle Paul. Infirmities were illnesses, reproaches were insults or being put down, needs were anything needed for survival, persecutions were hurts from others because he was a Christian, and distresses were incurable illnesses or problems for which he did not have any answer. Apostle Paul realized that Satan was trying to weaken his faith, and when he saw this, he let Holy Spirit put to use the Dunamis Power in his life. The result was that, by going through and being delivered from these problems, the faith of the Apostle Paul became stronger. So, it is with you, Born Again Christians. Satan will bring difficult things upon you spiritually and physically in an attempt to weaken your faith. Still, when you permit Holy Spirit to apply Dunamis Power to these problems, your faith will always become stronger.

John 6:2
(King James Version)
2 And a great multitude followed him, because they saw his miracles which he did on them that were diseased.

When Your Lord touched people who were sick, virtue or Dunamis Power flowed out of Him, and the people were instantly healed. As a result, many people saw blind people suddenly see, lame people suddenly walk, deaf people suddenly hear, and people who could not speak suddenly speak. These miracles occurred when Your Lord used spiritual rather than natural laws to heal the people.

Revelation 13:14
(King James Version)
14 And deceiveth them that dwell on the earth by the means of those miracles which he had power to do in the sight of the beast; saying to them that dwell on the earth, that they should make an image to the beast, which had the wound by a sword, and did live.

Revelation 16:14
(King James Version)
14 For they are the spirits of devils, working miracles, which go forth unto the kings of the earth and of the whole world, to gather them to the battle of that great day of God Almighty.

Revelation 19:20
(King James Version)
20 And the beast was taken, and with him the false prophet that wrought miracles before him, with which he deceived them that had received the mark of the beast, and them that worshipped his image. These both were cast alive into a lake of fire burning with brimstone.

2 Thessalonians 2:9
(King James Version)
9 Even him, whose coming is after the working of Satan with all power and signs and lying wonders,

Since Satan is a very deceptive person, he can do false or pretend miracles. However, he also possesses the ability to perform real miracles. He still has the same Dunamis Power that angels have as they minister to you and engage in spiritual warfare on your behalf. Now, note something very important. There is a limitation to the miracles Satan can do. He can only perform miracles in the physical and material realms; he cannot perform miracles in the spiritual realm. For example, Satan cannot use spiritual laws to save a person when one decides to become a born-again Christian. Only Your Lord could do that for a person, as He applies Dunamis Power to him or her through the spiritual laws of Our Father. Also, any miracle that Satan may do will only have a temporary positive effect. He is trying to destroy your spiritual being by attacking your physical body. One of his methods is to do a miracle, and then if one begins to trust in him because of the miracle, very soon he will begin to add pain and hurt to the person's life.

HUMAN MINDS AND SPIRITUAL MINDS

Let's talk more about how Holy Spirit heals the minds of human beings on the earth. There is one big difference between the minds of human beings and the minds of those who live in the spirit realm that must be reviewed to understand what I'm about to say. In the spirit realm, they function without the quality of time; therefore, their minds function without the concept of time. This means that when they think of an event, they think of what you call the past, present, and future of an event all at once. How does your mind work? In this natural world, we live with the quality of time. Therefore, when I think of an event, I not only think about the present of the event, but also the past and the future. I recall what led up to an event, I think about how the event is based upon the past, and I also think about what future effects they will have on my life." "Some humans are remembering past hurts, abuses, and troubling events in their lives, and they would like to forget about some of these things. Do you know what would happen if they could remove these troubling memories from their minds?

Because we cannot think eternal thoughts and have the quality of time in our thinking, we have to think about the past, present, and future of an event so we can meaningfully move through it. You have learned that Our Father can remove the memory of a sin from His mind after He forgives you of a sin. Our human mind cannot remove thoughts from our memory. Sometimes we joke about becoming forgetful as we age, but what's actually happening is that our ability to recall memories slows down. Therefore, if you experience hurtful and troubling events, you will always have a memory of these past events.

For example, I heard the story of a man who had an affair that lasted six weeks, then he stopped the affair, told his wife about it, and asked for her forgiveness. She told me that she forgave him, but she couldn't forget what he had done. She also planned to have an affair of her own so that her thoughts would have some balance about the matter in her mind. Both the husband and the wife have memories they will not forget in their earthly lives. He will always remember the enjoyment and the feeling of guilt of his affair. Even though she eventually forgave her husband, she will always remember the hurt when she heard about her husband's affair, and the guilt from having an affair that she did not enjoy. The husband and wife manage to live together, but it is very difficult with these memories in mind.

If the husband and wife had been willing to become born-again Christians, there is a healing that Holy Spirit could have brought about in their minds. Through the Gifts of Faith within them, he could have applied Dunamis Power, and though the memories are still in their minds, he could have suppressed the memories enough that they would not have recalled them very often. They would have still had these memories of the past used by Satan in trying to tempt them to make the same errors and sins again. However, when Born Again Christians have difficult memories, Holy Spirit can help so that these memories do not become a great problem for them. When you get to Heaven, you will be able to have all these difficult memories removed from your mind. The best guideline is for you not to do any sins that will leave troubling memories in your mind.

* * *

Chapter 14: Dunamis Power (Part 3)

Acts 7:38
(King James Version)
38 This is he, that was in the church in the wilderness with the angel which spake to him in the mount Sina, and with our fathers: who received the lively oracles to give unto us:

The worship of God's chosen people in Old Testament times was the Old Testament Church. The Sign of Circumcision was a law of Our Father to be followed for one to be part of the Old Testament Church. After the Resurrection of Your Lord, those of the Old Testament Church who became Born-Again Christians were the ones Your Lord used to start the New Testament Church, worshipping on the Lord's Day, which is Resurrection Sunday. "Eventually, some who were not Our Father's Chosen People began to become Born Again Christians and also part of the New Testament Church. Some of Our Father's Chosen People who were part of the New Testament Church began to say that for those who were not Our Father's Chosen People to be part of the New Testament Church, circumcision was necessary, as it was for the Old Testament Church. This resulted in a conflict in the New Testament Church over the matter of Circumcision. (See Acts Chapter 15.) Through Holy Spirit's leadership, the decision was made regarding those who were not Our Father's Chosen People and became Born Again Christians. They did not have to be circumcised to be part of the New Testament Church.

Our Father's People are still the Old Testament Church, even though they are living in the New Testament Church Age. Some of these are becoming Born-Again Christians and fall under the category of Messianic Our Father's Chosen People. Though the roles of those who are Our Father's Children and those who are not Our Father's Chosen People are reversed, the situation is very similar to Acts Chapter 15. There is a type of healing that can occur through Dunamis Power in the lives of Born-Again Christians who are not part of Our Father's chosen people. Born Again Christians who are not of Our Father's Chosen People can be made able to accept Our Father's Chosen People who become Born Again Christians as true believers in Your Lord's Church, even though it is more meaningful for them to continue to worship on the Sabbath Day rather than on the Lord's Day." My statement is not about whether the church in the wilderness is saved; it is about whether the church in the wilderness has become born again and now is part of the New Testament church, whether they should worship on Saturday, or what they call the Sabbath. Doing it on Saturday has more meaning for them, and it does not stop them from being part of the New Testament church.

1 Corinthians 6:3
(King James Version)

3 Know ye not that we shall judge angels? how much more things that pertain to this life?

JUDGING ONESELF

Holy Spirit had Apostle Paul write that Born Again Christians will judge angels. We will not judge all of the angels, and the judgment will be a special type of Judgment. We are going to judge the fallen angels, not the angels who did not become fallen angels. (See 2 Peter 2:4; Jude 6.) Actually, the judgment of these angels took place when they were cast out of Heaven and became fallen angels. After the Great Millennium, as the Great White Throne Judgment takes place for sinners, Born Again Christians will reaffirm the judgment made of the fallen angels when they were cast out of Heaven. Since Born Again Christians are great enough to be able to judge fallen angels, you should be able to make the necessary judgments that will enable you to overcome the differences that arise between and among you. In far too many situations, this is not happening. As in the time of the Apostle Paul, too many Born Again Christians were going to civil courts to resolve their differences rather than letting Holy Spirit help them resolve them through Dunamis Power. For example, some husbands and wives refuse to let their differences be resolved through Dunamis Power. What does that look like, one may ask, that is, allowing God's power to heal you where you need it, instead of going to civil court for a divorce. There are some Born-Again Christians who are suing each other over financial matters.

For Born-Again Christians, such differences should be settled or healed through the power of God. "There is one simple guideline that Holy Spirit thinks will help. Human beings, including many of you, Born Again Christians, are trying to settle your differences and disputes by judging who is right and who is wrong. For example, when something goes wrong in a home, the first instinct of the husband and wife is to blame the person they think is at fault. There should be a higher level of judging taking place. Rather than judging who is right and who is wrong, Born-Again Christians should be judging what is right and what is wrong. This would be based on the Ten Commandments rather than on people's personalities. One of Holy Spirit purposes is to extend Dunamis Power through the Gifts of Faith in Born Again Christians to resolve the differences and conflicts that arise between you and among you. If you base your judgments on what is right and wrong rather than who is right and wrong, then Holy Spirit will be able to lead you in every situation. "Satan can bring about differences and conflict among Born Again Christians when the Ten Commandments are not being totally followed. When two Born-Again Christians are involved in a conflict, in general, both are in error, not fully following the Ten Commandments. Usually, both Born Again Christians could judge the other one to be at fault. Therefore, rather than functioning on the level of accusation, both should be cooperative in allowing Holy Spirit to point out what is right in or for the situation, according to the Ten Commandments. He would do that by revelation to both of them if both would humble themselves.

DUNAMIS POWER USED AGAINST DEMONS

There is one very important thing that Christians need to learn, and that is to allow Holy Spirit to teach them how to use the Dunamis power given to them to cast out devils. Usually, when you have a drastic change of behavior and character, a demon is involved. The time to cast out demons in a person is when they are willing to surrender their life to Christ. In other words, when you are in the process of leading someone to Christ, you should be discerning whether there are any demons present that need to be dealt. When Christ was ministering on Earth, He always cast out demons from those who were possessed before extending to them the Gift of His Father's grace. Do not assume that demons will automatically leave when your Lord moves into the heart of a person. Usually, what happens is the demon or demons living in the spirit of the person will keep that person from making the proper decision to be able to accept Christ as their Personal Savior.

Matthew 8:16
(King James Version)
16 When the even was come, they brought unto him many that were possessed with devils: and he cast out the spirits with his word, and healed all that were sick:

Luke 4:40
(King James Version)
40 Now when the sun was setting, all they that had any sick with divers diseases brought them unto him; and he laid his hands on every one of them, and healed them.

Our Father's Chosen People did not feel free to bring their sick ones to the Lord until after sunset on the Sabbath Day. When the people brought their sick ones to the Lord, first He cast the demons out of those who were demon-possessed, and then He healed them. The reason for this is that one who is demon-possessed cannot accept Your Lord as his or her Personal Savior. The time to cast out demons is right before one receives the Gift of Our Father's Grace.

Matthew 10:1
(King James Version)

10 And when he had called unto him his twelve disciples, he gave them power against unclean spirits, to cast them out, and to heal all manner of sickness and all manner of disease.

Luke 10:17
(King James Version)
17 And the seventy returned again with joy, saying, Lord, even the devils are subject unto us through thy name.

Mark 16:17
(King James Version)
17 And these signs shall follow them that believe; In my name shall they cast out devils; they shall speak with new tongues;

When Your Lord called His twelve disciples, and when others following them became His disciples, Your Lord gave each one of you the power to cast out demons, then, when your witness gives Holy Spirit an opportunity to lead them to accept Your Lord as their personal Savior, if there are any possessing and hindering demons, that is the time for you to cast them out.

Acts 16:18-19
(King James Version)
18 And this did she many days. But Paul, being grieved, turned and said to the spirit, I command thee in the name of Jesus Christ to come out of her. And he came out the same hour.

19 And when her masters saw that the hope of their gains was gone, they caught Paul and Silas, and drew them into the marketplace unto the rulers,

```
When Apostles Paul and Silas cast the Demon of Divination
out of the young lady, she could no longer do
fortune-telling for profit. The demon was gone, and then the
young lady could receive the Gift of Our Father's Grace.
```

AUTHORITY IN CASTING OUT DEMONS

We have the authority to speak the word and cast out demons, but you realize it is actually the power of our Father, extended through you, that is really casting them out. Since demons are fallen angels, they have as much spiritual energy as angels do, but it is powered by darkness. When drained in spiritual warfare, they replenish it by feeding on the darkness created by human behavior or sin. The spirit energy they have is greater than the spirit light energy we have.

Numbers 13:26-30
(King James Version)
26 And they went and came to Moses, and to Aaron, and to all the congregation of the children of Israel, unto the wilderness of Paran, to Kadesh; and brought back word unto them, and unto all the congregation, and shewed them the fruit of the land.
27 And they told him, and said, We came unto the land whither thou sentest us, and surely it floweth with milk and honey; and this is the fruit of it.
28 Nevertheless the people be strong that dwell in the land,

and the cities are walled, and very great: and moreover we saw the children of Anak there.
29 The Amalekites dwell in the land of the south: and the Hittites, and the Jebusites, and the Amorites, dwell in the mountains: and the Canaanites dwell by the sea, and by the coast of Jordan.
30 And Caleb stilled the people before Moses, and said, Let us go up at once, and possess it; for we are well able to overcome it.

Patriarch Moses sent twelve spies, one man from each of the twelve tribes, into the Promised Land to assess the possibility of possessing it. All twelve reports stated that the land would be a great and plentiful place to live; however, the majority were negative and the minority were positive. Ten reported that the army of our father was not equipped to overcome the tall soldiers and fortified cities in the land. Two of the men, Joshua and Caleb, reported that since it was our Father's plan for them to have the land if they went into the land, he would give it to them. They had faith in the authority of our Father, and if they went into the land, he would help them cast out the demons in the land.

Isaiah 6:2
(King James Version)
2 Above it stood the seraphims: each one had six wings; with twain he covered his face, and with twain he covered his feet, and with twain he did fly.

One of the reasons that the Seraphim covered his face as he worshipped Our Father was that he recognized the Authority of Our Father. In recognizing the authority of Our Father, he was willing to do whatever Our Father commanded. The Seraphim ministered the same recognition to Prophet Isaiah, who said to Our Father, 'Here am I, send me.' All angels recognize the Authority of Our Father in whatever they do.

1 Corinthians 11:10
(King James Version)
10 For this cause ought the woman to have power on her head because of the angels.

Holy Spirit had Apostle Paul write to the women in the Church of Corinth that they were to cover their heads when in Church to recognize the Authority of their Fathers in their lives through the priestly roles of their husbands. Not only women, but all Born Again worshippers should be recognizing the Authority of Our Father when they are worshipping, as the angels recognize the Authority of Our Father when they worship. If I need to cast out a demon, I must realize that Our Father is actually the One in authority in the situation, not me." This is also why it is essential for you to live a holy life if you are to cast out demons. You can speak the necessary words to cast out demons, but it is only Dunamis Power that Holy Spirit extends through the Gift of Faith in you that is greater than the demon you want to cast out. Holy Spirit can best extend the Dunamis Power through a life that is holy according to the standards of the Bible.

AUTHORITY AND DEMONS

Matthew 8:16
(King James Version)
16 When the even was come, they brought unto him many that were possessed with devils: and he cast out the spirits

with his word, and healed all that were sick:
Luke 4:40-41

(King James Version)
40 Now when the sun was setting, all they that had any sick with divers diseases brought them unto him; and he laid his hands on every one of them, and healed them.
41 And devils also came out of many, crying out, and saying, Thou art Christ the Son of God. And he rebuking them suffered them not to speak: for they knew that he was Christ.

When the Lord was ministering on Earth, He had the authority and Dunamis Power to cast out demons.

Matthew 10:1
(King James Version)
10 And when he had called unto him his twelve disciples, he gave them power against unclean spirits, to cast them out, and to heal all manner of sickness and all manner of disease.

Luke 10:17
(King James Version)
17 And the seventy returned again with joy, saying, Lord, even the devils are subject unto us through thy name.

Mark 16:17
(King James Version)

17 And these signs shall follow them that believe; In my name shall they cast out devils; they shall speak with new tongues;

I wanted to repeat these verses of Scripture. All who become a disciple of Your Lord, that is, become a born-again Christian, receive the authority to cast out demons. That is, you have the authority to say the words necessary to cast out demons, which gives Holy Spirit the opportunity to use his Dunamis Power in casting out the demons.

Acts 5:16
(King James Version)
16 There came also a multitude out of the cities round about unto Jerusalem, bringing sick folks, and them which were vexed with unclean spirits: and they were healed every one.

In the ministry of the Apostle Peter, demons were cast out of many people so that the people could then be healed.

Acts 8:7
(King James Version)
7 For unclean spirits, crying with loud voice, came out of many that were possessed with them: and many taken with palsies, and that were lame, were healed.

When Deacon Philip ministered in the city of Samaria, demons were cast out of many people so that they could be healed.

One of Holy Spirit's challenges to the Church today is to continue to cast out demons so that people can receive the Gift of Our Father's Grace.

* * *

Chapter 15: Dunamis Power (Part 4)

Would you be afraid when you are involved in casting out demons? Some Born Again Christians have been taught that if they are not very careful, the demon or demons that are being cast out may attack them. Of course, we know that when it comes to certain things, people assume, and we also remember the story of the seven sons of Sheva who tried to cast out the spirit from a man. However, what actually happens is that when a spirit is cast out, the angels come, put a net around it, and take it away. The angels detain a demon that has been cast out for seven days. This gives the person in whom the demon used to reside seven days to invite Our Lord into their heart. When the demon returns later, it will not stay because that person's heart is not empty.

Matthew 12:43-45
(King James Version)
43 When the unclean spirit is gone out of a man, he walketh through dry places, seeking rest, and findeth none.

44 Then he saith, I will return into my house from whence I came out; and when he is come, he findeth it empty, swept, and garnished.
45 Then goeth he, and taketh with himself seven other spirits more wicked than himself, and they enter in and dwell there: and the last state of that man is worse than the first. Even so shall it be also unto this wicked generation.

Revelation 3:20
(King James Version)
20 Behold, I stand at the door, and knock: if any man hear my voice, and open the door, I will come in to him, and will sup with him, and he with me.

Note that the returning demon does not enter the heart of a person who is filled with the person of Christ. Since only Born-Again Christians are involved in the casting out of demons, this means that any demons cast out of the heart of a person will not enter the heart of a Born-Again Christian. Therefore, Born Again Christians do not need to be afraid of the demons when they are involved in or observe the casting out of demons. You can permit them to harass you if you have sin in your life, if one is cast out, possibly if you are present.

Matthew 10:26-31
(King James Version)
26 Fear them not therefore: for there is nothing covered, that shall not be revealed; and hid, that shall not be known.
27 What I tell you in darkness, that speak ye in light: and what ye hear in the ear, that preach ye upon the housetops.
28 And fear not them which kill the body, but are not able to kill the soul: but rather fear him which is able to destroy

both soul and body in hell.
29 Are not two sparrows sold for a farthing? and one of them shall not fall on the ground without your Father.
30 But the very hairs of your head are all numbered.
31 Fear ye not therefore, ye are of more value than many sparrows.

The meaning of the word fear in these verses means to be afraid of someone or something that is a danger to you. In these verses, your Lord taught that there are some persons and things that you, born-again Christians, should not fear. 1) You should not be afraid of those who persecute you. 2) You should not be afraid of Satan, demons, people, or things that can hurt your physical bodies. 3) You should not be afraid that Our Father would not provide for your needs in your life. There is only one thing Your Lord taught you to fear. He taught you to fear the quality of Our Father that will oversee the going to Hell of those who do not accept Your Lord as Messiah. Both their souls and bodies will go to Hell and suffer. This will be a time of eternal suffering.

JOY AND CELEBRATION

Remember, we taught that one of the angels' assignments is to maintain an atmosphere of heaven around you, so that the Dunamis power of our Father can continue to flow to you. Because of that, angels celebrate every night in your home because our Father is happy about two things. He is happy because you are a born-again Christian, and when you leave this earthly life, you will go to Heaven. He is also happy every day when you continue to refuse to worship the idols that Satan tempts you to worship. There are basically three things Satan uses to tempt you to idol worship. 1) Satan uses the passions and desires of your human body, 2) Satan uses false doctrines about the Bible, 3) Satan uses evil things in the world. Satan's game plan is to have you make some of these things more important than your worship and commitment to Our Father. Whenever you resist any of these temptations to do idol worship, angels rejoice and celebrate. Remember, we taught you that humans have events and parties, but heaven has celebrations.

This type of celebration always weakens Satan and the demons. This celebration in Heaven helps the angels to continue to be victorious in the spiritual warfare that is always taking place in the Heavenlies above you. Born Again Christians should also be rejoicing in their worship times and in their daily lives. The beginning of your celebration and rejoicing should center around one thing. Right now, you should be rejoicing that if this were the day that your life on Earth ceases, you would go to Heaven. This type of rejoicing will always weaken any demons nearby. A joyful atmosphere maintains a heavenly atmosphere.

Luke 15:6-10
(King James Version)

6 And when he cometh home, he calleth together his friends and neighbours, saying unto them, Rejoice with me; for I have found my sheep which was lost.
7 I say unto you, that likewise joy shall be in heaven over one sinner that repenteth, more than over ninety and nine just persons, which need no repentance.
8 Either what woman having ten pieces of silver, if she lose one piece, doth not light a candle, and sweep the house, and seek diligently till she find it?
9 And when she hath found it, she calleth her friends and her neighbours together, saying, Rejoice with me; for I have

found the piece which I had lost.
10 Likewise, I say unto you, there is joy in the presence of the angels of God over one sinner that repenteth.

```
These verses are about rejoicing or celebrating that takes
place in Heaven when one person on Earth becomes a
born-again Christian. The expression in the presence of the
angels has a very special meaning. This is about the angels
in Heaven observing Our Father as He celebrates and rejoices
when a person on Earth becomes a born-again Christian.
```

Luke 10:20
(King James Version)
20 Notwithstanding in this rejoice not, that the spirits are subject unto you; but rather rejoice, because your names are written in heaven.

Doing the ministry that Our Father has called you to do is very important. There should be some rejoicing about this, but this is not to be the basis of your rejoicing or celebrating. For example, some people may say to you or state in your presence that if they had a ministry like yours, they would be rejoicing or celebrating about it. If the size, type, or result of one's ministry were the basis of rejoicing, then Born Again Christians would be doing different amounts of rejoicing. The size, type, and result of your ministry is not to be the basis of your rejoicing, but the basis of your celebrating is knowing that if you were to leave this earthly life today, you would go to Heaven. This type of rejoicing will weaken Satan and any demons in the Heavenlies above you or may be close by where you are.

HEALING AND CLEANSING

New Testament Christians understand the matter of healing better, and the Old Testament, the matter of cleansing. Old Testament believers had a deeper understanding of spiritual cleanliness. For the Old Testament believers, this was more a matter of ceremonial cleansing, but there is something for you, New Testament Christians, to learn.

Numbers 5:1-5
(King James Version)
5 And the Lord spake unto Moses, saying,
2 Command the children of Israel, that they put out of the camp every leper, and every one that hath an issue, and whosoever is defiled by the dead:
3 Both male and female shall ye put out, without the camp shall ye put them; that they defile not their camps, in the midst whereof I dwell.
4 And the children of Israel did so, and put them out without the camp: as the Lord spake unto Moses, so did the children of Israel.
5 And the Lord spake unto Moses, saying,

Our Father gave Patriarch Moses the following instructions. If it was confirmed that a person had leprosy, the person was to live outside the camp. Those with leprosy lived in an isolated group, and they could not touch or fellowship with their families, their Church, or society. There were two reasons for this. 1) It was a matter of disease control. 2) It was also a matter of controlling spiritual defilement. If one touched a leper, the one who did the touching would also be considered to be spiritually unclean.

Leviticus 14:1-7
(King James Version)

14 And the Lord spake unto Moses, saying,
2 This shall be the law of the leper in the day of his
cleansing: He shall be brought unto the priest:
3 And the priest shall go forth out of the camp; and the
priest shall look, and, behold, if the plague of leprosy be
healed in the leper;
4 Then shall the priest command to take for him that is to be
cleansed two birds alive and clean, and cedar wood, and
scarlet, and hyssop:
5 And the priest shall command that one of the birds be
killed in an earthen vessel over running water:
6 As for the living bird, he shall take it, and the cedar wood,
and the scarlet, and the hyssop, and shall dip them and the
living bird in the blood of the bird that was killed over the
running water:
7 And he shall sprinkle upon him that is to be cleansed from
the leprosy seven times, and shall pronounce him clean, and
shall let the living bird loose into the open field.

If a person with leprosy was healed, two things needed to happen. 1) The priest would pronounce the person healed. 2) Then the priest would ceremonially cleanse the person, and then the person could resume contact with family, Church, and society.

Mark 1:42
(King James Version)

42 And as soon as he had spoken, immediately the leprosy

departed from him, and he was cleansed.

When your Lord ministered to the man with leprosy, two things happened at the same time. 1) The leprosy left the man, that is, a miracle healed him. 2) The man was cleansed. The only reason Your Lord told the man to go to the priest for the ceremony to become clean was so the people could know that the man was cleansed. When your Lord forgives a person for a moral sin, that person is spiritually clean from that point in time, not after a period of spiritual rehabilitation. This speaks sharply against some teachings introduced into the church today, which require penance. When you repent of sin, you are clean, and if you have gotten sick as a result of that sin, according to the word, you can be healed then. Only in rare circumstances do you have to tell someone of your sin. I'm attempting to show you the importance of using the Dunamis power of our Father, not just for yourselves but to minister to others. When it comes to compassion, one person actually feels some of another person's suffering. As a priest on earth, the Lord is attempting to teach us to follow in his footsteps, both in the past and in the present.

RELEASING COMPASSION THROUGH DUNAMIS POWER

Your Lord experienced every kind of suffering humans experience during His life and the event of His crucifixion. Therefore, when the Godhead shares compassion with humans, they are experiencing every suffering that any human may experience. If a person is not born again and doesn't have the gift of faith, the only way our Father can share his compassion with them is through another believer. The lord's compassion comes out of him in different ways and for different purposes, such as healing power, miracle-working power, or as an emotional sustaining power, etc. "It is a little different with angels. They have never lived in a human body like Christ did, so they have not experienced the suffering that our human bodies endure. In their spiritual warfare with demons, they experience every suffering you experience in your spirit beings. They experience all the sufferings that humans experience in their spirits, souls, emotions, and minds. They share compassion in these areas when they are ministering to you.

On the one hand, humans have the potential to share more compassion with other humans than angels because we live in human bodies and experience the suffering that comes with them. However, there is a reason why you do not. In the human part of you, you can develop immunity to feeling the repeated pains of suffering, especially in your human body. This is so that those who are not born-again Christians and do not have the Gift of Faith in them can endure the sufferings coming from living on Earth. As humans develop immunity to the pain of suffering, you share a lesser level of compassion than the angels. Saying it another way, our fallen nature cheats us of our ability to do deep ministry like our lord and the angels. Remember, part of sharing compassion is carrying one's pain, thereby lessening theirs.

Galatians 6:2
(King James Version)
2 Bear ye one another's burdens, and so fulfil the law of Christ.

Again, Compassion is helping another person by feeling some of the suffering they are experiencing. Probably, you should never tell another person, I know exactly what you are feeling.' It would be more accurate to say, 'I only know a little of what you are experiencing, but

I want to help you." Compassion is based upon the fellowship of two spirit beings. Thus, two Born Again Christians can share compassion, an angel and a Born-Again Christian can share compassion, and Our Father, Christ, and Holy Spirit can share compassion with angels and Born-Again Christians.

Psalm 23:4
(King James Version)
4 Yea, though I walk through the valley of the shadow of death, I will fear no evil: for thou art with me; thy rod and thy staff they comfort me.

In this Psalm, Holy Spirit uses the parable of a good shepherd to describe Our Father's care for His children. Our Father's care includes compassion for all your times of suffering and sorrow. In this verse, a sheep in a dark valley is a sheep that is not sensing the leadership and care of a shepherd. You know from experience that when humans enter a state of sorrow, they feel, at first, like sheep without a shepherd. Usually, you do not know what you are really feeling, or not feeling, and you do not know what to do. Our Father wants to share His compassion with you in times like that.

Psalm 116:16
(King James Version)
16 O Lord, truly I am thy servant; I am thy servant, and the son of thine handmaid: thou hast loosed my bonds.

When I preached the services for my loved ones going home, I began to experience what this verse meant.

1 Corinthians 15:55
(King James Version)
55 O death, where is thy sting? O grave, where is thy victory?

> For a born-again Christian, his or her physical death is always a time of victory. It is winning the race.

We hear great testimonies of people powerfully healed and delivered of drugs, alcohol, and many such things, who are experiencing our Father's grace. But do you know there is a higher level of grace we have yet to receive? When angels refused to sin in Heaven, unlike those who became fallen angels, they began to live at a level of God's grace that kept them from sinning. Angels have free will choice like humans do, but they are living on the level of Grace, where Grace keeps them from sinning. When you get to Heaven, you will also be living in the level of Grace, where Grace keeps us from sinning. Even though you will still have the potential to sin, our Father will keep you from sinning, as he is now keeping the angels from sinning. So, a greater testimony is our father keeping you from sinning, rather than being delivered from some great sin.

Our Father's grace that you received with your Gift of faith includes several things. Our Father's Grace includes faith, hope, love, and salvation from sin. Angels experience all of these areas of Our Father's Grace except one part of salvation, the forgiveness of sin. This means that because humans have a weakness to sin, Our Father relates to humans on a lower level of Grace than He does the angels. One other way that you will become like the angels when you get to Heaven is that you will experience Our Father's Grace on the higher level of Grace, where His Grace will keep you from doing any sinning throughout eternity." Our Father is a God of Pleasure, that is, happiness and joy. Because of this quality of Our Father, He created angels and humans to be recipients of His Pleasure, His happiness, and joy. In the Old Testament, Holy Spirit used the word favor to describe Our Father's Pleasure, and in the New Testament, the word Grace.

Revelation 4:7-11
(King James Version)
7 And the first beast was like a lion, and the second beast like a calf, and the third beast had a face as a man, and the fourth beast was like a flying eagle.
8 And the four beasts had each of them six wings about him; and they were full of eyes within: and they rest not day and night, saying, Holy, holy, holy, Lord God Almighty, which was, and is, and is to come.
9 And when those beasts give glory and honour and thanks to him that sat on the throne, who liveth for ever and ever,
10 The four and twenty elders fall down before him that sat on the throne, and worship him that liveth for ever and ever, and cast their crowns before the throne, saying,
11 Thou art worthy, O Lord, to receive glory and honour and power: for thou hast created all things, and for thy pleasure they are and were created.

Saints in Heaven and also the angels are singing about the Grace of Our Father. In this verse, Holy Spirit reports that they are singing about the glory of Our Father because of His Pleasure or will, His happiness, and joy. He created them. In Heaven, the angels are singing about Our Father's

Grace as much as humans are. (Revelation 5:8-14.)

Romans 6:1
(King James Version)
6 What shall we say then? Shall we continue in sin, that grace may abound?

Ephesians 2:8
(King James Version)
8 For by grace are ye saved through faith; and that not of yourselves: it is the gift of God:

Sinning did not and does not put the Grace of Our Father into operation. Grace is a gift from Our Father because He is a person of Good Pleasure. The only thing that sin brings is the wrath and judgment of Our Father.

Psalm 84:11
(King James Version)
11 For the Lord God is a sun and shield: the Lord will give grace and glory: no good thing will he withhold from them that walk uprightly.

This is an example of how in the Old Testament, Holy Spirit had a Hebrew word used that is translated as " favor or grace to describe the Pleasure quality of our Father."

* * *

VII

VII. The Prosperity of Spiritual Qualities

pros·per·i·ty
/präˈsperədē/

the condition of being successful or thriving

spir·it·u·al
/ˈspirəCH(əw)əl/

relating to or affecting the human spirit or soul as opposed to material or physical things.

Chapter 16: The Prosperity of Spiritual Qualities

We have been discussing faith and its various aspects, as they pertain to how our father gave it to us, zeroing in on the last two qualities of faith the power that flows through it and makes what heaven gives us possible. Now we want to turn the corner and examine some of the things that faith creates, if I can put it that way. This is all that most people used to hear about regarding faith in what I call the faith movement, which I refer to as the prosperity message, 'name it and claim it,' and healing.

There are three viewpoints on the topic of faith and prosperity: some believe that one of Our Father's great desires is to prosper His children financially. During the faith movement, this was the primary message preached, which only increased the spirit of greed within the church. Some believe that wanting more than your needs being supplied is allowing Satan to tempt you with greed. Some believe that financial prosperity is a proper Biblical teaching as long as, Born Again

Christians, do not place more emphasis upon financial prosperity than you do spiritual matters in your lives. In this lesson, I won't say which viewpoint is right, but I want to try to communicate in such a way that Holy Spirit can give you direction on whatever prosperity viewpoint you feel is proper Biblical teaching.

Psalm 84:11
(King James Version)
11 For the Lord God is a sun and shield: the Lord will give grace and glory: no good thing will he withhold from them that walk uprightly.

The expression no good thing is a translation of the Old Testament word favor. Also, remember that in the New Testament, the same meaning is conveyed by the word 'grace'. The meaning is that Our Father will not withhold any happy thing from you. In other words, Our Father is a person who is prosperous in happiness, and He wants, Born Again Christians, to be prosperous in happiness. "It should also be noted that Born Again Christians are spirit beings living in physical bodies. Therefore, Our Father wants you to be prosperous in happiness in your spirits and souls, including your emotions. He also wants you to be prosperous in happiness in your physical bodies. You already know that what gives you real happiness in your bodies is not the same thing that gives you real happiness in your spirits and souls.

Psalm 34:8
(King James Version)
8 O taste and see that the Lord is good: blessed is the man that trusteth in him.

Psalm 106:1

(King James Version)
106 Praise ye the Lord. O give thanks unto the Lord; for he is good: for his mercy endureth for ever.

Psalm 119:68
(King James Version)
68 Thou art good, and doest good; teach me thy statutes.

The word translated as "good" in these verses is a term that encompasses the meaning of happiness. These are only three of the verses in the Bible that state that Our Father is prospering in good (happiness) and He wants you to prosper in good (happiness). Keep in mind some of the things we have taught about angels, the rankings are only about doing the responsibilities angels have in an orderly and disciplined way: You have equal position or worth in the presence of Our Father." When you become saints in Heaven, you become like the angels. The saints in Heaven are pure, light beings, much like the angels. Now note this. The saints in Heaven have an equal position or worth with the angels as they worship with the angels before Our Father in Heaven. The prosperity of Happiness is one of the important parts of the Dunamis power of God, so is prospering in worship. Neither of these types of prosperity depends upon how much money a person has.

THE PROSPERITY OF WORSHIP

Luke 19:28-48
(King James Version)
28 And when he had thus spoken, he went before, ascending
up to Jerusalem. 29 And it came to pass, when he was come
nigh to Bethphage and Bethany, at the mount called the
mount of Olives, he sent two of his disciples, 30 Saying, Go

ye into the village over against you; in the which at your entering ye shall find a colt tied, whereon yet never man sat: loose him, and bring him hither.31 And if any man ask you, Why do ye loose him? thus shall ye say unto him, Because the Lord hath need of him.32 And they that were sent went their way, and found even as he had said unto them.33 And as they were loosing the colt, the owners thereof said unto them, Why loose ye the colt?34 And they said, The Lord hath need of him.35 And they brought him to Jesus: and they cast their garments upon the colt, and they set Jesus thereon.36 And as he went, they spread their clothes in the way.37 And when he was come nigh, even now at the descent of the mount of Olives, the whole multitude of the disciples began to rejoice and praise God with a loud voice for all the mighty works that they had seen;38 Saying, Blessed be the King that cometh in the name of the Lord: peace in heaven, and glory in the highest.39 And some of the Pharisees from among the multitude said unto him, Master, rebuke thy disciples.40 And he answered and said unto them, I tell you that, if these should hold their peace, the stones would immediately cry out.41 And when he was come near, he beheld the city, and wept over it,42 Saying, If thou hadst known, even thou, at least in this thy day, the things which belong unto thy peace! but now they are hid from thine eyes.43 For the days shall come upon thee, that thine enemies shall cast a trench about thee, and compass thee round, and keep thee in on every side,44 And shall lay thee even with the ground, and thy children within thee; and they shall not leave in thee one stone upon another; because thou knewest not the time of thy visitation.45 And he went into the temple, and began to cast out them that sold

therein, and them that bought;46 Saying unto them, It is written, My house is the house of prayer: but ye have made it a den of thieves.47 And he taught daily in the temple. But the chief priests and the scribes and the chief of the people sought to destroy him,48 And could not find what they might do: for all the people were very attentive to hear him.

I will explain why this Triumphal Entry of Jesus is an example of Prosperity of Worship. The people were able to put aside any differences or prejudices so that, as one group, they could worship Jesus. Humans do have prejudices that keep us apart. There are some prejudices among us humans because of the different races of people, and there are some prejudices because of the different groups of economic status among us. "There are even some prejudices in Our Lord's Church that keep Born Again Christians from worshipping together in unity. There are some differences about the meaning and method of Baptism that you cannot resolve. For example, some baptize by immersion, some by pouring water over one's body, and some by sprinkling. There are some differences about the meaning and method of Holy Communion that you cannot resolve. For example, some use fermented fruit of the vine and some unfermented fruit of the vine in the communion service. In some societies, you have the caste system, yet in others, men think they are better than women. Then you have others, due to their financial status, who think they are superior.

When saints worship together with angels in Heaven, all these differences and prejudices are not present. What the saints and angels realize as they worship together is that they have equal position or worth as they worship before Our Father. As, Born-Again Christians, begin to rise above the differences and prejudices that are keeping you apart, you enter into the Prosperity of Worship. The Prosperity of

Worship is the worship that takes place when Born Again Christians, though many, become the one earthly body of Your Lord."

Psalm 147:1
(King James Version)
147 Praise ye the Lord: for it is good to sing praises unto our God; for it is pleasant; and praise is comely.

In this verse, the word good is the happy quality of Our Father, and the word pleasant is when this happy quality of Our Father becomes a part of a human being. This happens in singing praises, that is, in worshipping Our Father. Prosperity of Worship is when the happiness of Our Father becomes a part of the life of the worshipper.

Psalm 92:1-4
(King James Version)
92 It is a good thing to give thanks unto the Lord, and to sing praises unto thy name, O Most High:
2 To shew forth thy lovingkindness in the morning, and thy faithfulness every night,
3 Upon an instrument of ten strings, and upon the psaltery; upon the harp with a solemn sound.
4 For thou, Lord, hast made me glad through thy work: I will triumph in the works of thy hands.

This is about worship on the Sabbath Day, now the Lord's Day. But the Lord's Day should not only be a day when a

```
Born-Again Christian refrains from work, but also worships
Our Father all day, from morning until night.
```

Ephesians 1:3
(King James Version)
3 Blessed be the God and Father of our Lord Jesus Christ, who hath blessed us with all spiritual blessings in heavenly places in Christ:

Ephesians 2:6
(King James Version)
6 And hath raised us up together, and made us sit together in heavenly places in Christ Jesus:

```
Heavenly places are not only about getting to Heaven
someday, but it is also about the Prosperity of Worship,
where a person is raised to Heavenly places in one's inner
spirit. This also includes a part of you being transported
there where he or she worships Our Father.
```

PROSPERITY OF HOPE

When you, as a Born-Again Christian, have a Prosperity of hope, you have very few disappointments in life. A disappointment is feeling let down or frustrated when what you expected did not happen. You can have a Prosperity of Hope, which can take these disappointments away

2 Thessalonians 2:16

(King James Version)
16 Now our Lord Jesus Christ himself, and God, even our Father, which hath loved us, and hath given us everlasting consolation and good hope through grace,

The word good in this verse is about the quality of good that is received from Our Father. Since the quality of goodness in Our Father includes the idea of prosperity, this verse refers to a Born-Again Christian having a quality of Prosperity of Hope. This is an eternal consolation or hope, as the ultimate goal of a born-again Christian on Earth is Heaven. Even if you have to prepare yourself to be a martyr, you can still hold on to prosperous hope. For Heaven will still be in your future. As long as your goal is Heaven, you can have prosperous hope. Notice this hope comes by the grace of our Father that flows to you through the gift of faith by his grace.

1 Corinthians 9:10-18
(King James Version)
10 Or saith he it altogether for our sakes? For our sakes, no doubt, this is written: that he that ploweth should plow in hope; and that he that thresheth in hope should be partaker of his hope. 11 If we have sown unto you spiritual things, is it a great thing if we shall reap your carnal things? 12 If others be partakers of this power over you, are not we rather? Nevertheless we have not used this power; but suffer all things, lest we should hinder the gospel of Christ. 13 Do ye not know that they which minister about holy things live of the things of the temple? and they which wait at the altar are partakers with the altar? 14 Even so hath the Lord ordained that they which preach the gospel should live of the gospel. 15 But I have used none of these

things: neither have I written these things, that it should be so done unto me: for it were better for me to die, than that any man should make my glorying void.
16 For though I preach the gospel, I have nothing to glory of: for necessity is laid upon me; yea, woe is unto me, if I preach not the gospel!
17 For if I do this thing willingly, I have a reward: but if against my will, a dispensation of the gospel is committed unto me.
18 What is my reward then? Verily that, when I preach the gospel, I may make the gospel of Christ without charge, that I abuse not my power in the gospel.

In this passage, Holy Spirit had Apostle Paul share from his own experiences. He shared his understanding that both those who plant the seed of the Gospel and those who harvest its fruit should do so in hope. Also, the Apostle Paul understood that those who preach the Gospel should receive their income for living from those who hear them preach. (Also see Matthew 10:10.) Holy Spirit also had Apostle Paul share his opinion on this matter. He believed that, since he could provide for his own needs through his trade, he should not take money for his living expenses from those to whom he preached the Word. Apostle Paul did not want to appear more concerned about the prosperity of material things than about the prosperity of spiritual things. On the one hand, Our Father's plan is still that those who preach the Gospel receive their income from those to whom they preach the Gospel. And on the other hand, Our Father agrees with the concern of Apostle Paul.

> For Born Again Christians who are preaching the Gospel, Our Father does not want it to appear that you are more concerned about material prosperity than you are spiritual prosperity.

* * *

Chapter 17: The Prosperity of Spiritual Qualities (Part 2)

When it comes to family, parents are the first line of defense against the spirit world. What is the greatest weapon the parents have for the child and against the enemy? It is love. I knew my parents loved me, but I couldn't remember many times when I was told. Children need to hear that they are loved consistently, and so do humans in general. It is from their parents that they learn what real love is, and only from born-again parents do they learn what God's kind of love is.

Psalm 100:5
(King James Version)
5 For the Lord is good; his mercy is everlasting; and his truth endureth to all generations.

Mercy is a part of love, and love is part of the goodness of Our Father. Since the word good includes the idea of prosperity, one of the meanings of this verse is that there is such a thing as the Prosperity of Love.

1 John 4:7-8
(King James Version)
7 Beloved, let us love one another: for love is of God; and every one that loveth is born of God, and knoweth God.
8 He that loveth not knoweth not God; for God is love.

It is important to note that Our Father is love, not that love is Our Father. The real quality of love is Our Father. Thus, a Born-Again Christian can have Prosperity of Love to the degree that one knows and has fellowship with Our Father.

BIBLICAL EXAMPLES OF LOVE

John 3:16
(King James Version)
16 For God so loved the world, that he gave his only begotten Son, that whosoever believeth in him should not perish, but have everlasting life.

The most important example is Our Father. He is so prosperous in His love that He can give His full love to all the angels and all who become born-again Christians. And Our Father also loves all other people, even though they do not return love to Him. Our father is the first example of love in the Bible.

Genesis 18:16-33

(King James Version)

16 And the men rose up from thence, and looked toward Sodom: and Abraham went with them to bring them on the way. 17 And the Lord said, Shall I hide from Abraham that thing which I do; 18 Seeing that Abraham shall surely become a great and mighty nation, and all the nations of the earth shall be blessed in him? 19 For I know him, that he will command his children and his household after him, and they shall keep the way of the Lord, to do justice and judgment; that the Lord may bring upon Abraham that which he hath spoken of him. 20 And the Lord said, Because the cry of Sodom and Gomorrah is great, and because their sin is very grievous; 21 I will go down now, and see whether they have done altogether according to the cry of it, which is come unto me; and if not, I will know. 22 And the men turned their faces from thence, and went toward Sodom: but Abraham stood yet before the Lord. 23 And Abraham drew near, and said, Wilt thou also destroy the righteous with the wicked? 24 Peradventure there be fifty righteous within the city: wilt thou also destroy and not spare the place for the fifty righteous that are therein? 25 That be far from thee to do after this manner, to slay the righteous with the wicked: and that the righteous should be as the wicked, that be far from thee: Shall not the Judge of all the earth do right? 26 And the Lord said, If I find in Sodom fifty righteous within the city, then I will spare all the place for their sakes. 27 And Abraham answered and said, Behold now, I have taken upon me to speak unto the Lord, which am but dust and ashes: 28 Peradventure there shall lack five of the fifty righteous: wilt thou destroy all the city for lack of five? And he said, If I find there forty and five, I will not

destroy it.29 And he spake unto him yet again, and said, Peradventure there shall be forty found there. And he said, I will not do it for forty's sake.30 And he said unto him, Oh let not the Lord be angry, and I will speak: Peradventure there shall thirty be found there. And he said, I will not do it, if I find thirty there.31 And he said, Behold now, I have taken upon me to speak unto the Lord: Peradventure there shall be twenty found there. And
he said, I will not destroy it for twenty's sake.32 And he said, Oh let not the Lord be angry, and I will speak yet but this once: Peradventure ten shall be found there. And he said, I will not destroy it for ten's sake.33 And the Lord went his way, as soon as he had left communing with Abraham: and Abraham returned unto his place.

Abraham had enough love that he could intercede in prayer for the wicked city of Sodom.

Genesis 37:25-28
(King James Version)
25 And they sat down to eat bread: and they lifted up their eyes and looked, and, behold, a company of Ishmeelites came from Gilead with their camels bearing spicery and balm and myrrh, going to carry it down to Egypt.
26 And Judah said unto his brethren, What profit is it if we slay our brother, and conceal his blood?
27 Come, and let us sell him to the Ishmeelites, and let not our hand be upon him; for he is our brother and our flesh. And his brethren were content.

28 Then there passed by Midianites merchantmen; and they drew and lifted up Joseph out of the pit, and sold Joseph to the Ishmeelites for twenty pieces of silver: and they brought Joseph into Egypt.

Joseph had enough love so that he could continue to love his brothers even though they sold him into slavery. Are you growing in love? It can be measured, you know.

Esther 8

(King James Version)

8 On that day did the king Ahasuerus give the house of
Haman the Jews' enemy unto Esther the queen. And
Mordecai came before the king; for Esther had told what he
was unto her.2 And the king took off his ring, which he had
taken from Haman, and gave it unto Mordecai. And Esther
set Mordecai over the house of Haman.3 And Esther spake
yet again before the king, and fell down at his feet, and
besought him with tears to put away the mischief of Haman
the Agagite, and his device that he had devised against the
Jews.4 Then the king held out the golden sceptre toward
Esther. So Esther arose, and stood before the king,5 And
said, If it please the king, and if I have favour in his sight,
and the thing seem right before the king, and I be pleasing
in his eyes, let it be written to reverse the letters devised by
Haman the son of Hammedatha the Agagite, which he wrote
to destroy the Jews which are in all the king's provinces:6
For how can I endure to see the evil that shall come unto my
people? or how can I endure to see the destruction of my

kindred?7 Then the king Ahasuerus said unto Esther the queen and to Mordecai the Jew, Behold, I have given Esther the house of Haman, and him they have hanged upon the gallows, because he laid his hand upon the Jews.8 Write ye also for the Jews, as it liketh you, in the king's name, and seal it with the king's ring: for the writing which is written in the king's name, and sealed with the king's ring, may no man reverse.9 Then were the king's scribes called at that time in the third month, that is, the month Sivan, on the three and twentieth day thereof; and it was written according to all that Mordecai commanded unto the Jews, and to the lieutenants, and the deputies and rulers of the provinces which are from India unto Ethiopia, an hundred twenty and seven provinces, unto every province according to the writing thereof, and unto every people after their language, and to the Jews according to their writing, and according to their language.10 And he wrote in the king Ahasuerus' name, and sealed it with the king's ring, and sent letters by posts on horseback, and riders on mules, camels, and young dromedaries: 11 Wherein the king granted the Jews which were in every city to gather themselves together, and to stand for their life, to destroy, to slay and to cause to perish, all the power of the people and province that would assault them, both little ones and women, and to take the spoil of them for a prey, 12 Upon one day in all the provinces of king Ahasuerus, namely, upon the thirteenth day of the twelfth month, which is the month Adar.13 The copy of the writing for a commandment to be given in every province was published unto all people, and that the Jews should be ready against that day to avenge themselves on their enemies.14 So the posts that rode upon

mules and camels went out, being hastened and pressed on by the king's commandment. And the decree was given at Shushan the palace. 15 And Mordecai went out from the presence of the king in royal apparel of blue and white, and with a great crown of gold, and with a garment of fine linen and purple: and the city of Shushan rejoiced and was glad. 16 The Jews had light, and gladness, and joy, and honour. 17 And in every province, and in every city, whithersoever the king's commandment and his decree came, the Jews had joy and gladness, a feast and a good day. And many of the people of the land became Jews; for the fear of the Jews fell upon them.

THE PROSPERITY OF LOVE

Esther had enough love for her people, Our Father's Chosen People, that she was willing to risk losing her life so that many of her people would not be killed.

Job 1:21-22
(King James Version)
21 And said, Naked came I out of my mother's womb, and naked shall I return thither: the Lord gave, and the Lord hath taken away; blessed be the name of the Lord.
22 In all this Job sinned not, nor charged God foolishly.

Job of the Old Testament had so much love for Our Father that even though he lost his children and possessions, He still worshipped Our Father.

Daniel 6:16

(King James Version)

16 Then the king commanded, and they brought Daniel, and cast him into the den of lions. Now the king spake and said unto Daniel, Thy God whom thou servest continually, he will deliver thee.

Daniel had so much love for our Father, even though this meant that he was placed in a lion's den, he was still faithful to Our Father.

Acts 7:60

(King James Version)

60 And he kneeled down, and cried with a loud voice, Lord, lay not this sin to their charge. And when he had said this, he fell asleep.

Deacon Stephen had so much love for Our Father that he forgave those who were stoning him to death as they were stoning him.

Genesis 37:3

(King James Version)

3 Now Israel loved Joseph more than all his children, because he was the son of his old age: and he made him a coat of many colours.

```
Jacob (Israel) did not have total Prosperity of Love. He
loved all of his children, but he loved his youngest son
more than the other eleven.
```

THE PROSPERITY OF TRUTH

Another area in which born-again Christians can be prosperous through their gift of faith is in the pursuit of truth. Did you know that there is a difference between scientific facts and truth? The way we experience the natural world around us is through the five physical senses our father gave us. Through these five senses, we humans experience our physical bodies and the natural world around us.' This is the realm where what humans refer to as scientific fact is in effect. These scientific facts help humans function through their five senses as they live in their physical body and the natural world around them.

Scientific facts do not help you as a spiritual being. Truth is what helps a spirit being. So, there is a difference between scientific facts and truth. Truth is more than a collection of knowledge of a group of scientific facts.

John 14:6
(King James Version)
6 Jesus saith unto him, I am the way, the truth, and the life: no man cometh unto the Father, but by me.

1 John 5:6
(King James Version)
6 This is he that came by water and blood, even Jesus Christ;

not by water only, but by water and blood. And it is the Spirit that beareth witness, because the Spirit is truth.

Since Christ Your Lord and Holy Spirit are actually of Our Father/Christ/Holy Spirit, these two verses mean that truth is Our Father/Christ/Holy Spirit. Truth, Our Father/Christ/Holy Spirit, is the only reality that exists. All other spirit beings, human beings, other life forms, and material things all come from Truth. Scientific facts are important, but they are not reality or Truth. The only Truth in existence is a Person, Our Father/Christ/Holy Spirit."

Genesis 2:7
(King James Version)
7 And the Lord God formed man of the dust of the ground, and breathed into his nostrils the breath of life; and man became a living soul.

When angels were created by Our Father, they were made to receive Truth and fellowship with It. Understand what I'm saying now, I'm not just making reference to information. I'm talking about God's very life itself, his spirit light energy. The only other beings that can receive Truth are human beings. When Our Father created the first human being, Adam, first He created a human body for Adam. Then, our Father created a living spirit and placed the living spirit in the body of Adam. The living spirit was created in the likeness of Our Father, so that Adam could receive Truth and have fellowship with Truth. All human beings have been and are created in the likeness of Adam. When the first human, Adam, sinned, he could not receive Truth and lost fellowship with Our Father. Through the shed Blood of Christ, our Father restored human beings to the position of faith, where we can receive Truth and have fellowship with it. Then you begin to know Truth. (See John 8:32.)

When humans become born-again Christians, they begin to receive Truth and have fellowship with Truth. To the degree that you receive the Person of Truth into your lives and have fellowship with Him, you have Prosperity of Truth, or a lack of Prosperity of Truth. A time factor is involved in this. For example, to have meaningful fellowship with your wife, you must spend quality time with her.

> A Born Again Christian needs to spend all of his or her time with Holy Spirit and Christ, your Lord, and His Church if that one is to have a Prosperity of Truth." What is all my time you say? That is staying in fellowship.

* * *

Chapter 18: The Prosperity of Spiritual Qualities (Part 3)

Note: Angels understand the meaning of an enemy because they are engaged in spiritual warfare against enemies of Our Father, Satan, and demons. It is important to understand that Satan and demons choose to be our enemies, but angels do not choose to be the enemies of Satan and demons. Instead, they resist Satan and demons because of what they are trying to do to destroy what Our Father is accomplishing. Angels do not choose Satan and demons as their enemies, because that would mean they would have to hate them.

What am I saying? If someone chose to hate you and begin to act that way, and you begin to evaluate them as your enemy. You will soon begin to feel hatred toward that individual. That hate will then begin to destroy your inner peace. To maintain your peace, you cannot choose to be the enemy of someone, nor can you evaluate them to be your enemy. Therefore, even though I know there are some people who choose to be my enemy, I do not choose to be the enemy of anyone.

I recognize those who choose to be my enemies as people who are opposed to me rather than people who are my enemies. I may resist one who opposes me, but not with any hate. If I were to begin to hate such a person, then I would be choosing that one to be my enemy.

THE PROSPERITY OF PEACE

The Prosperity of Peace is not something that will bring about the cessation of wars on Earth. This will not happen until the Great Millennium. There is the fear of a terrorist attack all around us, but you can't become afraid. I know that I am at peace with Our Father, and if events were to destroy my physical body, I would immediately be in the presence of Our Father in Heaven.

James 4:4
(King James Version)
4 Ye adulterers and adulteresses, know ye not that the friendship of the world is enmity with God? whosoever therefore will be a friend of the world is the enemy of God.

John 2:15-17
(King James Version)
15 And when he had made a scourge of small cords, he drove them all out of the temple, and the sheep, and the oxen; and poured out the changers' money, and overthrew the tables;
16 And said unto them that sold doves, Take these things hence; make not my Father's house an house of merchandise.
17 And his disciples remembered that it was written, The zeal of thine house hath eaten me up.

Romans 8:7

(King James Version)
7 Because the carnal mind is enmity against God: for it is not subject to the law of God, neither indeed can be.

People who are sinners and those who are committing sins are enemies of Our Father, along with Satan and demons. When one becomes a Born-Again Christian, that one is no longer an enemy of Our Father. Born Again Christians, through their Gifts of Faith, receive the quality of peace from Our Father. The more individual Born-Again Christians remove sinful activities, sinful feelings, and sinful thoughts from his or her lives, the more prosperous they become in peace.

John 14:27
(King James Version)
27 Peace I leave with you, my peace I give unto you: not as the world giveth, give I unto you. Let not your heart be troubled, neither let it be afraid.

Since Our Father/Christ/Holy Spirit are one person, yet three persons living together in peace, Your Lord had a quality of peace that He could give to each one of His disciples. Holy Spirit has the same quality of peace that he can give to each one who becomes a born-again Christian. Those who receive the gift of peace from him are no longer enemies of Our Father and are at peace with their individual consciences. This peace becomes prosperous when Born Again Christians experience inner calm, even in the face of troubling events.

Ephesians 2:14-16
(King James Version)
14 For he is our peace, who hath made both one, and hath broken down the middle wall of partition between us;

15 Having abolished in his flesh the enmity, even the law of commandments contained in ordinances; for to make in himself of twain one new man, so making peace;
16 And that he might reconcile both unto God in one body by the cross, having slain the enmity thereby:

The peace that Holy Spirit gave to those Christians when the Church of Your Lord started enabled both Your Father's Chosen People and those not Your Father's Chosen People to be unified as the Body of Your Lord. This peace has the potential to enable all Born Again Christians living on Earth to function together in unity. The unity of believers is one result of the Prosperity of Peace.

THE PROSPERITY OF MEEKNESS

Matthew 5:5
(King James Version)
5 Blessed are the meek: for they shall inherit the earth.

The word earth refers to the land or ground of Planet Earth. In the Great Millennium, Born Again Christians will possess this land. This word also refers to the benefits received from the ground of Planet Earth. Note these two important things. First of all, these benefits come from Our Father as an inheritance. This means that Our Father divides His benefits for Planet Earth among His children, as a father or mother divides the benefits of their estate through the inheritance they give to their children. Secondly, our Father provides these benefits of Planet Earth through meekness that you receive from the measure and gift of faith you receive when you become a born-again Christian. What am I saying, like all the fruit of the spirit, you reap the benefits of those fruits by activating them through doing or walking in them, by or through the gift of faith given to you. Which is the measure of faith and the gift of faith given to you. This is why you need to cultivate the Prosperity of Meekness, as your parents did.

Leviticus 20:24
(King James Version)
24 But I have said unto you, Ye shall inherit their land, and I will give it unto you to possess it, a land that floweth with milk and honey: I am the Lord your God, which have separated you from other people.

Our Father told Patriarch Moses that when Our Father's Chosen People went into the Promised Land, they would possess the land as an inheritance from Our Father.

Joshua 3:9-17
(King James Version)
9 And Joshua said unto the children of Israel, Come hither, and hear the words of the Lord your God. 10 And Joshua said, Hereby ye shall know that the living God is among you, and that he will without fail drive out from before you the Canaanites, and the Hittites, and the Hivites, and the Perizzites, and the Girgashites, and the Amorites, and the Jebusites. 11 Behold, the ark of the covenant of the Lord of

***all the earth passeth over before you into Jordan. 12 Now
therefore take you twelve men out of the tribes of Israel, out
of every tribe a man. 13 And it shall come to pass, as soon as
the soles of the feet of the priests that bear the ark of the
Lord, the Lord of all the earth, shall rest in the waters of
Jordan, that the waters of Jordan shall be cut off from the
waters that come down from above; and they shall stand
upon an heap. 14 And it came to pass, when the people
removed from their tents, to pass over Jordan, and the
priests bearing the ark of the covenant before the people; 15
And as they that bare the ark were come unto Jordan, and
the feet of the priests that bare the ark were dipped in the
brim of the water, (for Jordan overfloweth all his banks all
the time of harvest,) 16 That the waters which came down
from above stood and rose up upon an heap very far from
the city Adam, that is beside Zaretan: and those that came
down toward the sea of the plain, even the salt sea, failed,
and were cut off: and the people passed over right against
Jericho. 17 And the priests that bare the ark of the covenant
of the Lord stood firm on dry ground in the midst of Jordan,
and all the Israelites passed over on dry ground, until all
the people were passed clean over Jordan.***

Notice again how Leader Joshua led the army of Our Father's Chosen People across the Jordan River into the Promised Land. The priest carrying the Ark of the Covenant went first with the army following. When the soles of the feet of the priest touched the water of the river, the water parted, and the army crossed the river on dry land. The city of Jericho was captured after the priests led a procession of worship around the city. When the priests and the army shouted in worship on the seventh day of seizing the city, through the power of Our Father, the walls of the city fell. All the army had to do was cleanse the land from spiritual uncleanness.

Because of their meekness, Our Father began to give them possession of the Promised Land as an inheritance. Then a problem developed. Some of Our Father's Chosen People began to worship other gods along with Our Father. Then some difficulties arose in their possession of the land as an inheritance because they no longer had the Prosperity of Meekness. Despite the problems, Our Father was able to divide the inheritance among the twelve tribes as He had planned. The prosperity of Meekness is important so that Our Father can give to you as an inheritance the prosperity of the material things of Planet Earth that He has planned for your earthly inheritance. Remember, blessed are the meek, for they shall inherit, so meekness is connected to receiving the things needed to prosper.

So far, we have talked about Prosperity of Happiness, Prosperity of Worship, Prosperity of Hope, Prosperity of Love, Prosperity of Truth, Prosperity of Peace, and Prosperity of Meekness. This shows that prosperity and faith are about much more than financial prosperity as I mentioned even though things are important when it comes to living on the earth. When you have a family, spending time with them is more important; in this way, you show the prosperity of compassion by meeting their physical and emotional needs.

COMPASSION

Hebrews 4:14-15
(King James Version)
14 Seeing then that we have a great high priest, that is passed into the heavens, Jesus the Son of God, let us hold

fast our profession.
15 For we have not an high priest which cannot be touched with the feeling of our infirmities; but was in all points tempted like as we are, yet without sin.

Christ, Your Lord, was willing to give up all the riches and luxuries He was enjoying in Heaven and come down to Planet Earth and live in a human body. He did this so that He could become the blood sacrifice for the forgiveness of the sins of all people and experience everything we humans experience in our bodies, minds, emotions, and spirits as we live on Earth. While living on Earth, the quality of compassion was more important to Him than any prosperity of material things. Christ, Your Lord, still has the Prosperity of Compassion. Our Father does not have any problem with a Born-Again Christian having prosperity of material things, but Our Father does become concerned when a Born-Again Christian becomes more concerned about the prosperity of material things than he or she is about his or her Prosperity of Compassion.

1 John 3:17-19
17 But whoso hath this world's good, and seeth his brother have need, and shutteth up his bowels of compassion from him, how dwelleth the love of God in him?
18 My little children, let us not love in word, neither in tongue; but in deed and in truth.
19 And hereby we know that we are of the truth, and shall assure our hearts before him.

When you see another person who you could help, you should share some of your worldly goods with them. But Our Father's plan is that you share the feelings of kindness and empathy in your heart along with your worldly goods. Compassion is more than giving money to another person; it is also about sharing yourself with that person. If you did not have any money to share, you could still share yourself.

How much money you share is not a measure of your compassion and love, nor is how much Our Father prospers you financially a measure of His compassion and love for you. Like our father, it's about giving as much of yourself as possible.

* * *

VIII

VIII. Prosperity Of Finances

fi·nance
/ˈfīˌnan(t)s,fəˈnan(t)s/

money or other liquid resources of a government, business, group, or individual

Chapter 19: Prosperity of Finances

Among Born Again Christians, there are differences of opinion about this. Some Christians understand the Holy Spirit to teach in the Bible that Christians are to be satisfied with their basic physical needs being met. Some teach that Our Father intends for Born-Again Christians to prosper financially, so that they have the means to spread the Gospel and feed the hungry. Some teach that it is okay to prosper financially as long as one's desire for money is not more important than seeking Our Father. Rather than explain which one of these viewpoints is the right one, I'm going to say a few things that are intended to help all Born Again Christians, regardless of their viewpoint, about financial prosperity. When I think of seed time and harvest, sowing and reaping in the area of finances. I think of weeds; just as in the ground, they can greatly hinder your finances as well.

3 John 2

(King James Version)

2 Beloved, I wish above all things that thou mayest prosper

and be in health, even as thy soul prospereth.

This verse was written by the Apostle John in a way that implies Our Father wants to bless Born-Again Christians with prosperity in material things and good health. The term prosperity of health is a proper term. It is important to note the little word, as in this verse. This means that something else must happen before a Born-Again Christian can prosper materially and maintain good health. The prosperity of one's soul should take place first. That is why we taught you about eight ways a Born-Again Christian can prosper in their soul, such as happiness, worship, hope, love, truth, peace, meekness, and compassion.

Psalm 85:12
(King James Version)
12 Yea, the Lord shall give that which is good; and our land shall yield her increase.

The word good refers to the spiritual blessing Our Father gives to His children from His good or happy heart. Our Father's plan is that when this happens, a child of Our Father can receive prosperous blessings from this land.

Matthew 13:22
(King James Version)
22 He also that received seed among the thorns is he that heareth the word; and the care of this world, and the deceitfulness of riches, choke the word, and he becometh unfruitful.

Some teach that if a Born-Again Christian sows a seed of faith offering into the ground of a good ministry, our Father will bless them with a prosperous harvest of material blessings. Before this could happen, the one who is planning to sow should have good ground or soil to receive the Word of Our Father. During the prosperity teaching of the 70s and 80s, the emphasis was placed on the ground one was sowing into rather than on the ground of the one sowing. But in the parable of your Lord that we refer to as the Parable of the Sower. If one receives the Word of Our Father and has some thistles (weeds) in his or her spirit, the Word of Our Father cannot grow in that one's inner being. Your Lord described the thistles or weeds as the deceitfulness of riches. What am I saying, giving money in the kingdom doesn't automatically trigger returns. It's the word of God growing in your spirit concerning giving that does, along with giving. Because again, you can be giving for the wrong reason, with the wrong mindset, or for the wrong purpose, which can make your ideas concerning money deceitful.

BE AWARE OF HUMAN NATURE

As one becomes prosperous, human nature tends to seek even greater prosperity. The problem is that it is easy for such a person to begin to forget that all the good material things do not in any way prepare them, so that when they experience physical death, they go to Heaven. Holy Spirit teaching in 3 John 1:2 is that as you let the seeds of spiritual prosperity grow in your spirits, one of the resulting fruits can be financial prosperity. Giving priority to spiritual prosperity keeps Satan from tempting one to be tempted by the deceitfulness of riches. This is the most crucial truth for Born-Again Christians to consider. Giving just to get by itself alone is not the formula for prosperity; in fact, it is seeking things, not the kingdom. Remember, as your soul prospers, it makes your seed good, which in turn makes your fruit good, which is financial prosperity. Not keeping the weeds out, which is sin, will hinder it.

Keep in mind something very important about prosperity and angels. It is through their help, with the guidance of the Holy Spirit, that it becomes possible. The spiritual qualities of prosperity that you receive strengthen the angels around you because they are spirit beings. As they are strengthened, one of the ways it blesses you is that they can use their wings, which are not used for flight but for ministry. Ministering to our Father and reflecting fiery darts from the enemy away from you. Financial prosperity may bless you as a human being, but any financial prosperity you have does nothing for your spirit light, being angels."

Deuteronomy 8:1-4
(King James Version)
8 All the commandments which I command thee this day shall ye observe to do, that ye may live, and multiply, and go in and possess the land which the Lord sware unto your fathers.
2 And thou shalt remember all the way which the Lord thy God led thee these forty years in the wilderness, to humble thee, and to prove thee, to know what was in thine heart, whether thou wouldest keep his commandments, or no.
3 And he humbled thee, and suffered thee to hunger, and fed thee with manna, which thou knewest not, neither did thy fathers know; that he might make thee know that man doth not live by bread only, but by every word that proceedeth out of the mouth of the Lord doth man live.
4 Thy raiment waxed not old upon thee, neither did thy foot swell, these forty years.

```
Deuteronomy teaches us here that one of the reasons our
father permitted this suffering in their life was to teach
them that they needed more than physical food to have a
meaningful life. The Ten Commandments were for the spiritual
part of their lives.
```

THE PROSPERITY OF MATERIAL THINGS

These verses also relate to our father's prosperity as he began to develop them into a nation. "First of all, it should be noted that the possibility of prosperity was present with the miracle manna. Our Father provided enough manna that His Chosen People could have gathered more than needed for their daily supply. Secondly, the prosperity of manna was given to the whole group of Our Father's Chosen People, the nation, or you could say, the Old Testament Church. The manna was on the ground around the encampment of more than two million people when they awakened each morning. Thirdly, a question has arisen that warrants serious consideration. The question was not; how much prosperity of manna did Our Father give to each family? But the question was, how much of the prosperity of manna that Our Father gave to the Old Testament Church could each family keep for themselves?

It is still a concern of Our Father with Born Again Christians. You still need a daily portion of the spiritual manna of His Word for meaningful lives. Our Father knows that humans have a tendency: once you begin to enjoy material things, you want more to enjoy. The danger is that some may begin to give more priority to enjoying the prosperity of material things than they do to daily eating the spiritual manna of His

Word.

John 4:32-34
(King James Version)
32 But he said unto them, I have meat to eat that ye know not of.
33 Therefore said the disciples one to another, Hath any man brought him ought to eat?
34 Jesus saith unto them, My meat is to do the will of him that sent me, and to finish his work

When Christ Your Lord was living on Planet Earth, He was more concerned about spiritual food than He was physical food.

Revelation 2:17
(King James Version)
17 He that hath an ear, let him hear what the Spirit saith unto the churches; To him that overcometh will I give to eat of the hidden manna, and will give him a white stone, and in the stone a new name written, which no man knoweth saving he that receiveth it.

As long as a Born-Again Christian is living in a physical body on Planet Earth, that one should give priority to the hidden manna, that is, both the Living and Written Word." Our Father's plan is that every Born-Again Christian in Your Lord's New Testament Church leaves their children a spiritually prosperous heritage, which is more important than leaving them money. This began in the Old Testament church when our Father initiated the manna miracle in Israel's life. Learning to depend on our father more than material things is of the utmost importance, especially in these last days. Israel had much gold in the wilderness, but that gold could not feed them.

Acts 7:38
(King James Version)
38 This is he, that was in the church in the wilderness with the angel which spake to him in the mount Sina, and with our fathers: who received the lively oracles to give unto us:

The angels observed a time in the Church when there were neither rich nor poor. As you recall, during those forty Years in the wilderness, neither their clothes nor their shoes wore out. Through daily miracles, Our Father provided the prosperity of manna for their food. But, as you recall, the instruction from Our Father was for each man to gather daily the amount of manna that was needed for the needs of his family. During those forty Years, there were not some who were poor because they had less than others, and there were not any who were rich because they had more than others." In the present day, I hear many Bible teachings about receiving financial prosperity from Our Father if one sows a seed of faith offering in a good ministry. The result is that some in Our Lord's Church have more financial prosperity than others. Isn't this a little different than the pattern Our Father established with His Chosen People during the forty Years in the wilderness when they began the Old Testament Church.

It should be noted again that in these teachings on financial prosperity, I am not stating which Bible interpretation of financial prosperity is correct. I am trying to state some guidelines that will speak to all viewpoints of financial prosperity.

What changes did Our Father make concerning the food supply for His Chosen People when they entered into the Promised Land?" The only change Our Father made was the source of the food supply. After they were in the Promised Land, there was no more manna for food. They ate from the produce of the land. Evidently, the people did not continue to follow the guidelines of taking only what each family needed from the food supply's prosperity. Soon, there were some poor people and some rich people. For example, when Christ Our Lord was on Planet Earth, He spoke frequently about the poor and the rich. When did our Father's Chosen People of the Old Testament Church stop following the plan Our Father gave them when they were traveling the forty years in the wilderness?

It is one basic factor that brought about the change. They continued to worship Our Father, but also at times they worshipped other gods. When they needed money to buy idols and items of idol worship (see Genesis 31:19-35), they began to take more from material prosperity than what they needed to meet their daily needs. "Our Father does give financial prosperity to Born Again Christians, Our Lord's Church. There are a few important factors Our Father wants you to keep in mind. First of all, Our Father is the owner of everything on Planet Earth. Humans are the stewards, not the owners. (See Genesis 1:28, Psalm 50:10-11.) Secondly, the covenant of prosperity is one Our Father made with His Old Testament Church, not with the individual people in it. (See Deuteronomy 29:1, 9, 2 Chronicles 24:20, Nehemiah 2:20.) Thirdly, when Our Father shares financial prosperity to Your Lord's Church through one of you are Born Again believers, that one should always be seeking Holy Spirit's guidance about how much of that prosperity Our Father wants that person to keep for themselves no so much as to how much show I give.

* * *

Chapter 20: Prosperity of Finances (Part 2)

John 6:7
(King James Version)
7 Philip answered him, Two hundred pennyworth of bread is not sufficient for them, that every one of them may take a little.

Before Christ Our Lord, through a miracle, fed five thousand people, some of His disciples discussed with Christ Our Lord whether or not they should spend two hundred ***denarii*** for buying bread for the crowd. Well, if you do calculations from today's dollars, a ***denarius*** was the average day's pay for a worker during the time Your Lord was on Earth. Based upon working five days a week, and a salary of $30,000.00 a year, if you were to calculate the equivalent in today's pay for two hundred days of work. According to my calculation, the amount of money would be close to $24,000.00. If the disciples were carrying this amount of money with them, it means that there was some prosperity involved with your Lord and His disciples.

Matthew 8:20
(King James Version)
20 And Jesus saith unto him, The foxes have holes, and the birds of the air have nests; but the Son of man hath not where to lay his head.

Even though prosperity was available to Christ Our Lord, He did not spend much of the money on Himself. For example, Holy Spirit reminded me that Christ Our Lord taught us that the birds and the foxes have homes, but that Christ Our Lord did not buy a home for Himself. There is a very important question every Born-Again Christian should ask when Our Father gives some prosperity or money through that person to Our Lord's Church. The question is, is there any of this money that Our Father wants me to use on myself, and if so, how much?' I know this is not taught, but this is how giving should be approached.

Luke 19:8
(King James Version)
8 And Zacchaeus stood, and said unto the Lord: Behold, Lord, the half of my goods I give to the poor; and if I have taken any thing from any man by false accusation, I restore him fourfold.

The rich man Zacchaeus is another Bible example to consider. When this rich man became a born-again Christian, he made some decisions about the prosperity of the money he had. Holy Spirit said Zacchaeus realized that the money was actually God's and that he needed to decide how much to keep for himself. Holy Spirit said He directed the Born-Again Zacchaeus to make the following decision about his financial prosperity. First of all, Holy Spirit helped him to decide to give one-half of his prosperity to the poor. Secondly, while serving as a tax collector, he became wealthy by collecting the prescribed taxes, by collecting more than the prescribed amount through deceit, and by investing his money. Holy Spirit helped him decide to give back fourfold any money he had gained through deceit while serving as a tax collector. He had him think about a law of retribution in Exodus 22:1. He led Zacchaeus to return to the person from whom he had deceitfully taken tax money, four times the amount he had taken by deceit.

ONLY LET GOD PROSPER YOU

Psalm 73:12
(King James Version)
12 Behold, these are the ungodly, who prosper in the world; they increase in riches.

Job 12:6
(King James Version)
6 The tabernacles of robbers prosper, and they that provoke God are secure; into whose hand God bringeth abundantly.

Born Again Christians should also be aware that Our Father is not the only one who can see that people prosper financially – Satan can help those who worship him or follow him to prosper financially. You should always be living a life of faith and holiness so that you do not give Satan any opportunity to prosper you financially. You should only receive financial prosperity when it comes from Our Father.

I recall one year when I cut a seed potato into pieces. Each piece had to have an eye or a place with a sprout. I would place the potato pieces in the ground, and several months later, I would dig the new potatoes. There would always be from six to eight new potatoes from each piece of seed potato planted in the ground. Something happened between planting the potato seed and digging the new potatoes. A small potato plant would start to grow into a large plant, bloom, and then a few weeks later, the plant would die." It is important to notice that the piece of seed potato produced the plant, but it was the plant that produced the potatoes for the harvest.

```
There is yet another important aspect to consider regarding
financial prosperity. Some teach that sowing seeds can
result in financial prosperity. The sowing of seed that Holy
Spirit wrote about in the Bible is for the purpose of the
salvation of souls. The sowing of seeds is about the saving
of souls.
```

REAPING WHAT YOU HAVE SOWED

Matthew 13:18
(King James Version)
18 Hear ye therefore the parable of the sower.

This verse is from the Parable of the Sower. The meaning of the parable is that as a Born-Again Christian, you are to be good soil into which Our Father can sow the seed of His Word. Then you are to become a plant growing in the good soil. As a plant, you are to produce fruit for a harvest. That is, the life you live and the witness you speak are to become fruit that, when people receive (eat) this fruit, they will become a born-again Christian. In this parable, the increase from the seed is the fruit of your life and witness as a born-again Christian. The increase in this parable is not about financial prosperity, but about the prosperity of Our Father's Word in your life." Let me say it another way, the lord plants Himself inside of you as seed. You, in turn, plant the word of God into the life of someone else. The result of the lord planting himself in you is now producing not only in your life but also in the lives you are now planting.

John 4:36-37
(King James Version)
36 And he that reapeth receiveth wages, and gathereth fruit unto life eternal: that both he that soweth and he that reapeth may rejoice together.
37 And herein is that saying true, One soweth, and another reapeth.

When you read the two previous verses of Scripture before this parable, you realize that this is about a born-again Christian, sowing the seed of Our Father's Word that you have received into your life. In the Parable of the Sower, Our Father sows the seed of His Word into your life. In this parable, you sow the seed of Our Father's Word into the lives of others. This is something that all Born Again Christians should be doing. Sometimes you will reap a harvest from the seed of Our Father's life you sow into the lives of other people. But usually, you will be reaping a harvest of souls from the seed of Our Father's Word that other Born Again Christians have sown into the lives of people. There is a prosperity increase among Born Again Christians who sow the seed of Our Father's Word, because the lives and witness of each one will result in several people becoming Born Again Christians.

SOULS AND MONEY ARE NOT THE SAME

In order to receive financial prosperity, you are to give gifts of money and material things. It is not the same as sowing seeds of Our Father's Word for a harvest of souls.

Luke 6:38
(King James Version)
38 Give, and it shall be given unto you; good measure, pressed down, and shaken together, and running over, shall men give into your bosom. For with the same measure that ye mete withal it shall be measured to you again.

The last part of the verse is about using an honest measure. The parable that Christ, your Lord, used was that of a farmer giving some grain or fruit to someone. The bosom is the part of the cloak between the shoulders that the farmer wore. The cloak was so designed that the farmer could fill this area of his cloak with grain and fruit and carry it to some place. Christ Your Lord taught that if the farmer gave away the amount of grain or fruit to someone, Our Father would see that the farmer would receive in return more than he had given away.

The word "give" that Holy Spirit used in this verse is not the word for "sow"; it means "to give a gift." A gift is something you give to another person, without expecting anything in return. So, this is different than sowing seeds and expecting a harvest.

Proverbs 19:17
(King James Version)
17 He that hath pity upon the poor lendeth unto the Lord; and that which he hath given will he pay him again.

Proverbs 28:27
(King James Version)
27 He that giveth unto the poor shall not lack: but he that hideth his eyes shall have many a curse.

Giving to the poor is one way that you give to Our Lord's Church. When you give in this manner, you are actually lending money to Our Father. And, when Our Father pays back the money you loan to Him, He will pay with interest.

1 Corinthians 9:10-11
(King James Version)
10 Or saith he it altogether for our sakes? For our sakes, no doubt, this is written: that he that ploweth should plow in hope; and that he that thresheth in hope should be partaker of his hope.
11 If we have sown unto you spiritual things, is it a great thing if we shall reap your carnal things?

In these two verses, Holy Spirit states that Our Father gives two things to Born Again Christians who are faithful in doing things Our Father's way. First of all, He supplies the seeds of His Word for Bom Again Christians to sow. When the seeds of His Word are sown, there is a prosperity harvest of souls. Secondly, Our Father supplies food. He supplies for your needs through the efforts of your hands. Remember, when Our Father's Chosen People entered the Promised Land, they no longer ate manna from Heaven, but they ate the produce of the land. When you give gifts of money to Your Lord's Church, Our Father responds with financial prosperity so that you can give more gifts of money to Your Lord's Church.

I have been trying to make a distinction between sowing seeds of Our Father's Word for a harvest of many people becoming Born Again Christians and giving gifts of money to Our Lord's Church for ministry. Why is Holy Spirit emphasizing the giving of money to Our Lord's Church rather than sowing seed faith offerings in Our Lord's Church?" The concern of Our Father is the temptation of greed. Sowing seeds of Our Father's Word for a prosperity harvest of souls does not have the potential of being a temptation to greed. Giving a gift is not a temptation to greed, because you give it without expecting anything in return. If you expect something in return, then it is not a gift.

It is this teaching concerning faith, giving seed for ministry, sowing seed faith offering, and when the seeds of his word are sown for the prosperity of souls that have been all poured into one pot, that has produced the abuse of prosperity in the church, using scriptures that were never intended to be used for finances. In this teaching, taking a different look at faith, we have taught that you were given a natural Quality of Faith when you were born, you received a Measure of Faith when you became a Born-Again Christian, and you received a Gift of Faith when Christ our Lord baptized you in the HS Spirit. The purpose of these qualities of faith that you have is to enable you to have a person-to-person, intimate fellowship with the Godhead. The way Our Father planned for you to receive financial prosperity is to give gifts of money to Christ Your Lord's Church. Let's take a look at a few more scriptures.

Jeremiah 9:23-24
(King James Version)
23 Thus saith the Lord, Let not the wise man glory in his wisdom, neither let the mighty man glory in his might, let not the rich man glory in his riches:

24 But let him that glorieth glory in this, that he understandeth and knoweth me, that I am the Lord which exercise lovingkindness, judgment, and righteousness, in the earth: for in these things I delight, saith the Lord.

```
You are not to glory in Your financial prosperity: You are
to glory in understanding and knowing Our Father. The word
understanding means intellectual understanding of Our
Father. The word know means for you to know the ways of Our
Father. These become a source of glory for you when you
understand, and your knowing results in a person-to-person
relationship with Our Father.
```

Philippians 3:8
(King James Version)
8 Yea doubtless, and I count all things but loss for the excellency of the knowledge of Christ Jesus my Lord: for whom I have suffered the loss of all things, and do count them but dung, that I may win Christ,

The word things: meaning the things of Earth, which include money, is what Apostle Paul disdained after he developed a person-to-person relationship with Our Father/Christ/Holy Spirit; he no longer gave any priority to the things of this world. For Apostle Paul, he knew he needed some money and things for survival, but beyond that, he so devalued the things of this world that they were like useless things to be thrown away. Apostle Paul was concerned about making a generous offering to the Church in Jerusalem for the poor. He did not give any priority to having personal financial prosperity.

Our Father is not suggesting a pattern for all Born Again Christians in these lessons about money. He suggests that all Born Again Christians should have serious discussions with Holy Spirit.

* * *

IX

IX. Testing The Qualities of Faith

testing
/ˈtestiNG/

the action or process of testing or checking someone or something to reveal a person's capabilities by putting them under strain; challenging.

Chapter 21: Testing The Qualities of Faith

This chapter is about the Testing of the Qualities of Faith in you. When I tore my rotator cuff years ago, I had to go through what they called physical therapy, where the surgical muscles go through rigorous tests for strength training so that resistance does not set in, where the muscles need to move freely. In a very real sense, the Qualities of Faith in born-again Christians are spiritual muscles within you. From time to time, Our Father will give you greater spiritual responsibilities to do for the purpose of strengthening your Qualities of Faith.

Acts 3:1-10

(King James Version)

3 Now Peter and John went up together into the temple at
the hour of prayer, being the ninth hour. 2 And a certain
man lame from his mother's womb was carried, whom they
laid daily at the gate of the temple which is called Beautiful,
to ask alms of them that entered into the temple; 3 Who
seeing Peter and John about to go into the temple asked an

alms. 4 And Peter, fastening his eyes upon him with John, said, Look on us. 5 And he gave heed unto them, expecting to receive something of them. 6 Then Peter said, Silver and gold have I none; but such as I have give I thee: In the name of Jesus Christ of Nazareth rise up and walk. 7 And he took him by the right hand, and lifted him up: and immediately his feet and ankle bones received strength. 8 And he leaping up stood, and walked, and entered with them into the temple, walking, and leaping, and praising God. 9 And all the people saw him walking and praising God: 10 And they knew that it was he which sat for alms at the Beautiful gate of the temple: and they were filled with wonder and amazement at that which had happened unto him.

Apostles Peter and John had such compassion for the lame man that they wanted to give him an offering. Remember, this man lay there every time the disciples and your Lord walked into this temple. On this particular occasion, their compassion went out to the lame man, but they did not have any money. Their compassion was so great that they had to do something for the man. So they exercised their faith, and it grew as they prayed for the man, and he was healed. From time to time, Our Father gave Apostles Peter and John greater things to do in their ministries, and their faith grew and developed. You are also aware of the results. Apostle Peter had a great healing ministry. Apostle John had such a close, personal relationship with Christ that Christ gave him a vision that became the Book of Revelation in your Bible. Holy Spirit will always give Born Again Christians greater things to do, strengthening their Qualities of faith. There will be times when you will have spiritual responsibility and feel totally inadequate to fulfill it. But if you go ahead and start doing it, Holy Spirit will help you, and your faith will become stronger as you do. As we always teach and now bear witness to, our father, through the written and spoken word, will consistently lead us through life and ministry, challenging us to act on our promptings to strengthen our faith muscles spiritually. Our failure to be a doer cripples us and our growth.

HE TESTS YOUR FAITH

This is about our Father helping you test your faith under many different circumstances. First of all, there are some things that Our Father has created into the order and Patterns of Planet Earth that result in you having to wait for some things to happen. For example, during the night, you have to wait for the sunrise to see the sun again. There is a plan of growth and maturity that Our Father has built into all life forms, which results in you waiting for things to happen. When I plant my garden, I have to wait about two months for the plants to grow and let them ripen. When you were a child, you began waiting for several years before you became an adult. This waiting develops patience and endurance in the three types of Qualities of Faith within you. The examples I provided help you develop qualities of patience and endurance, which in turn strengthen your faith. You see how our Father put the mechanisms in place to help you, even though you had not really started your spiritual life.

Secondly, there are times when you ask Our Father for something in prayer, and He delays answering. The reason for this is that the timing of your receiving the answer to your prayer is as important as the answer to your prayer. You only have memories of your past and know only the present of the life you are experiencing. Our Father knows not only the past and present of your life, but also the future. So, Our Father has a better understanding of when the answer to your prayer would not only bless you but also do for Christ Your Lord's

Church what Our Father intends the blessing to do. Remember, this is not just about you, but we are all connected.

John 11:6
(King James Version)
6 When he had heard therefore that he was sick, he abode two days still in the same place where he was.

When Christ, Your Lord, heard that His friend, Lazarus, was sick and dying, He was about twenty-five miles away. Christ Your Lord deliberately delayed His departure so that Lazarus would be dead four days when He arrived. The two sisters of Lazarus asked why He did not come in time to heal their brother. Then Christ, Your Lord, raised Lazarus from the dead. The raising from the dead of Lazarus better prepared Christ Your Lord's disciples and the sisters of Lazarus for the soon coming Resurrection of Christ Your Lord, more than a miracle healing of Lazarus would have prepared them. God has a purpose for everything he does or allows.

Daniel 9:21
(King James Version)
21 Yea, whiles I was speaking in prayer, even the man Gabriel, whom I had seen in the vision at the beginning, being caused to fly swiftly, touched me about the time of the evening oblation.
Daniel 10:13
(King James Version)
13 But the prince of the kingdom of Persia withstood me one and twenty days: but, lo, Michael, one of the chief princes, came to help me; and I remained there with the kings of Persia.

Even though Satan was able to delay Our Father's answer to Daniel's prayer for twenty-one days, the answer arrived at the time Our Father wanted the answer to arrive. The delay actually strengthened Daniel's faith qualities for the task ahead of him. Brothers and sisters, tests and trials with our Father are all about getting you ready and getting you ready for what's next. With the devil, it is always about hindrances, stopping you, changing you, or killing you.

TEMPTATIONS THAT ARE ALLOWED

There is a type of temptation that Our Father permits Satan to do to Born Again Christians now and then for the purpose of testing how well you are disciplining your moral living. This type of temptation is to try to get you to satisfy a physical desire of your body in a way that is not suggested by Holy Spirit in the Bible, regardless of what that is. The technique that Satan uses is one that he uses very often. He tries to convince Born Again Christians that there are little times of lack of discipline of the feelings of your physical body, if you go ahead and do it, doing the little thing will not hurt you or your Christian Faith. "One important thing to keep in mind is that what you refer to as habits is a part of disciplining the physical feelings of your bodies in the way Our Father desires you to discipline your feelings.

Now, note an important way in which Our Father created humans. He created you so that, through your subconscious mind, you can begin to react to pain before you are consciously aware of it. Through habits, you help your mind function in this positive manner. I make this statement quite often that all truths are parallel. Which means if you can form natural habits, you can form spiritual ones. But this also means that when Satan tempts you to satisfy a feeling in your body in a way that is not Scriptural, you can start to avoid doing the temptation even before you are aware it is happening. If every time you are aware that Satan is tempting you to some type of lustful expression that is not Biblical, and you refuse to do it, you are forming a good habit in that situation. Thus, when Satan tempts you, you will start to resist the temptation even before you begin to think about it. If you would do one little lustful thing that Satan tells you is small and would not hurt you, you would start a trend in your habits that will hinder your ability to resist a temptation before you are consciously aware it is happening." This is a very important and powerful truth.

Hebrews 4:15
(King James Version)
15 For we have not an high priest which cannot be touched with the feeling of our infirmities; but was in all points tempted like as we are, yet without sin.

Since Christ Your Lord was tempted in every way that you are ever tempted while He was living on Planet Earth, this means that the desires of the physical body in which He was living received the same temptations that your body receives.

Matthew 4:4-11
(King James Version)
4 But he answered and said, It is written, Man shall not live by bread alone, but by every word that proceedeth out of the mouth of God.5 Then the devil taketh him up into the holy city, and setteth him on a pinnacle of the temple,6 And saith unto him, If thou be the Son of God, cast thyself down: for it is written, He shall give his angels charge concerning thee: and in their hands they shall bear thee up, lest at any time

thou dash thy foot against a stone.7 Jesus said unto him, It is written again, Thou shalt not tempt the Lord thy God.8 Again, the devil taketh him up into an exceeding high mountain, and sheweth him all the kingdoms of the world, and the glory of them;9 And saith unto him, All these things will I give thee, if thou wilt fall down and worship me.10 Then saith Jesus unto him, Get thee hence, Satan: for it is written, Thou shalt worship the Lord thy God, and him only shalt thou serve.11 Then the devil leaveth him, and, behold, angels came and ministered unto him.

This happened right after the Baptism of Christ, Your Lord, and the first temptation Satan gave Christ Your Lord is an example of the topic of this lesson. After forty days of fasting from food, the physical body of Christ, Your Lord, had extreme feelings of hunger. Satan tried to get Christ, Your Lord, to eat some food a short time before Our Father intended for Him to again eat food. Satan tried to get Christ, Your Lord, to obtain the food in a way other than Our Father intended. Through faith and the Word, Christ Your Lord did not give in to the temptation of Satan that time or any other time. "In order to strengthen your faith, Our Father is going to permit Born Again Christians to be tempted in this manner as long as you are living in your physical bodies on Earth.

```
If you permit Holy Spirit to do so, through the Gift of
Faith that he has given to you, Holy Spirit can give you the
desire and power to resist any temptation Satan can put
before you. You should never have to say, 'Satan made me do
it.'
```

ANOTHER TYPE OF TEMPTATION

There is a type of temptation that Satan uses, of which I want to alert you. Sometimes, when a person begins to pray for people and healing results from the prayers, Satan tries to make that person feel that the healing occurred because of something they did. Sometimes Satan will try to get the person to feel that he or she is some type of special Christian with a special gift because a healing takes place when the person prays. This is a temptation to resist. "When Born Again Christians are praying for the healing of other people, the Gift of Faith becomes the instrument through which the power of Our Father goes to the one being healed. Electricity flowing through an electric wire is a good parable example. Born Again Christians are not to take any of the glory when healings take place. This diminishes the value of the Gift of Faith. First of all, you are to live a holy life. Secondly, when a healing occurs through your prayers, you should recognize that your commitment to Our Father has brought you to the right place at the right time for the healing to take place.

Romans 4:19-21
(King James Version)

19 And being not weak in faith, he considered not his own body now dead, when he was about an hundred years old, neither yet the deadness of Sarah's womb:20 He staggered not at the promise of God through unbelief; but was strong in faith, giving glory to God;21 And being fully persuaded that, what he had promised, he was able also to perform.

There was a time in the lives of Patriarch Abraham and his wife that they needed a miracle. They were both too old physically to produce or beget together a son, Our Father promised. Patriarch Abraham knew that his own abilities would have nothing to do with the birth of such a son. What did he do? He gave the glory to Our Father. How did he give the glory to Our Father? He believed a son was going to be born because of the Promises or Word of Our Father. In the same way, if you really believe that when a healing takes place when you pray, that it happens because of the Promises and Word of Our Father, you will not take any of the glory of the healing for yourself. This is very important to understand. For when people pray for the healing of others and healing take place, Satan will always begin to tempt the one who does the praying. Satan will try to get that person to begin to believe that he or she has some special importance in the mind of Our Father because the healing took place. Or Satan will try to get the person to feel that he or she has some special type of gift. In this way, Satan tries to get people to misuse the Gift of Faith." This will be a great problem in the lives of the youth that our Father will use in the great awakening that is about to happen. "In these closing days of the Age of Our Father's Grace, it is important for all Born Again Christians to be disciplining their lives so that they either begin their days or end their days with an hour of worship and prayer.

There is one type of temptation that Satan is trying to get Born Again Christians to do that would hinder them in disciplining their lives in this manner. This is not about Satan tempting you to do something bad. This is about Satan tempting you in the matter of doing good things. There are many good things that Our Father wants Born Again Christians to be doing in their Churches and their ministries. Our Father calls you to do good things, but Satan tries to get you doing so many good things that you do not have much time for daily worship and prayer. Our Father will not call you to do so many good things in your Church or your ministry that you do not have much time left for daily worship and prayer.

The Natural faith that Our Father placed in you when you were born in your mother's womb, the Measure of faith Our Father gave you when you became a Born Again Christian, and the Gift of Faith Our Father gave you when Christ Your Lord baptized you in (HS) all need the spiritual nourishment of you praying and worshipping at least one hour each day. These elements of faith function best when nourished with a daily hour of worship and prayer."

Luke 22:39

39 And he came out, and went, as he was wont, to the mount of Olives; and his disciples also followed him.

John 18:2

(King James Version)

2 And Judas also, which betrayed him, knew the place: for Jesus ofttimes resorted thither with his disciples.

Because Christ Your Lord prayed every day, many people knew where He would be when He was praying and when He would be praying. Accordingly, because Christ Your Lord was praying near Jerusalem, Judas knew where to find Christ Your Lord. Even when he was not in Jerusalem, He had daily times for prayer.

Luke 6:12

12 And it came to pass in those days, that he went out into a mountain to pray, and continued all night in prayer to God.

Christ Your Lord went up into a mountain and prayed all night before He named His twelve disciples. Christ Your Lord was in a place of prayer, but He was also in communication with Our Father all night.

Mark 1:35

35 And in the morning, rising up a great while before day, he went out, and departed into a solitary place, and there prayed.

Christ, Your Lord, also prayed early in the morning before sunrise.

Matthew 14:2

23 And when he had sent the multitudes away, he went up into a mountain apart to pray: and when the evening was come, he was there alone.

Luke 5:16

16 And he withdrew himself into the wilderness, and prayed.

Luke 9:18

18 And it came to pass, as he was alone praying, his disciples were with him: and he asked them, saying, Whom say the people that I am?

Christ, Your Lord, often prayed alone. Again, I want to say that Christ Your Lord was never so busy preaching, teaching, and performing miracles that He did not have time to spend hours in prayer.

* * *

Also by Dr. Eugene Underwood

Building A Firm Foundation

Our Lord lays it out very clearly as to what must happen within one's soul for the kingdom of God to come fully within you. Two succeed there are two things you must know, there are two people trying to kill you, the devil and God. The devil wants to destroy the very existence of God within you and if he can't do that he will simply just try to kill you. God wants to destroy the self-life within you and if he's successful you will wish for the first one, that the devil would have killed you. This plan of the lord is brilliant; he knows we will experience tremendous suffering in this world because of the evil that is here. He incorporated it into your life to use it to bring about a death to the self- life, thereby you proving your worth of him the pearl of great price. Hence, the life of the overcomer, triumphing over sin at every turn and surrendering your life for his. It is about failing and passing test because you will fail some and triumph over others, thereby passing and being promoted.

Suffering Unto Perfection 1 : Beginning the Journey

The Suffering Series: I have watched for many years believers of different backgrounds and levels of spiritual growth, discard the importance of the Old Testament. Which is a great mistake that will bring dire consequences to many. Just as Israel journeyed from Egypt to the promised land it parallels the exact journey you and I are on as a believer. The stories of these heroes' lives reveal to us principles, laws, and doctrines of heaven and the ways of our Father.

Suffering Unto Perfection 2 : Three Phases of the Crucified Life

More of The Suffering Series

Suffering Unto Perfection 3 : Taking Back The Soul

More of The Suffering Series

Suffering Unto Perfection 4 : The Life Of Growth And Transformation

More of The Suffering Series

Suffering Unto Perfection 5 : Becoming Like Him

More of The Suffering Series

That We Might Be One

New roots are emerging in our day that will bring great destruction if the body of Christ does not intervene. The body of Christ must be one.

Worship

Whatever you are going through, you should be growing through, and worship releases the grace of our Father to make it possible. Worship is so many things to us. It brings purity, clarity, stability, and a deep longing for our Father.

www.ingramcontent.com/pod-product-compliance
Lightning Source LLC
LaVergne TN
LVHW050616100826
845148LV00011B/1605

9798986828268